Doctrine

by Asa Mahan

CONTENTS.

MORALLY RIGHT, OR WRONG.--Those who are and are not virtuous, how distinguished--Selfishness and Benevolence--Common Mistake--Defective forms of Virtue--Test of Conformity to Moral Principle--Common Mistake--Love as required by the Moral Law--Identity of Character among all Beings morally Virtuous

CHAPTER XII.

ELEMENT OF THE WILL IN COMPLEX PHENOMENA.--Natural Propensities--Sensation, Emotion, Desire, and Wish defined--Anger, Pride, Ambition, &c.--Religious Affections--Repentance--Love--Faith-- Convictions, Feelings and external Actions, why required or prohibited-- Our Responsibility in respect to such Phenomena--Feelings how controlled by the Will--Relation of Faith to other Exercises morally right

CHAPTER XIII.

INFLUENCE OF THE WILL IN INTELLECTUAL JUDGMENTS.--Men often voluntary in their Opinions--Error not from the Intelligence, but Will--Primary Faculties cannot err--So of the secondary Faculties--Assumptions-- Pre-judgments--Intellect not deceived in Pre-judgments--Mind, how influenced by them--Influences which induce false Assumptions--Cases in which we are apparently, though not really, misled by the Intelligence

CHAPTER XIV.

LIBERTY AND SERVITUDE.--Liberty as opposed to moral Servitude--Mistake of German Metaphysicians--Moral Servitude of the race

CHAPTER XV.

LIBERTY AND DEPENDENCE.--Common Impression--Spirit of Dependence--Doctrine of Necessity tends not to induce this Spirit--Doctrine of Liberty does--God controls all Influences under which Creatures act--Dependence on account of moral Servitude

CHAPTER XVI.

DEDICATORY PREFACE.

To one whose aim is, to "serve his generation according to the Will of God," but two reasons would seem to justify an individual in claiming the attention of the public in the capacity of an author--the existence in the public mind of a want which needs to be met, and the full belief, that the Work which he has produced is adapted to meet that want. Under the influence of these two considerations, the following Treatise is presented to the public. Whether the author has judged rightly or not, it is not for him to decide. The decision of that question is left with the public, to whom the Work is now presented. It is doubtful, whether any work, prepared with much thought and pains-taking, was ever published with the conviction, on the part of the author, that it was unworthy of public regard. The community, however, may differ from him entirely on the subject; and, as a consequence, a work which he regards as so imperiously demanded by the public interest, falls dead from the press. Many an author, thus disappointed, has had occasion to be reminded of the admonition, "Ye have need of patience." Whether the following Treatise shall succeed in gaining the public ear, or not, one consolation will remain with the writer, the publication of the work has satisfied his sense of duty. To his respected Associates in the Institution over which he presides, Associates with whose approbation and counsel the work was prepared, the Author would take this occasion publicly to express his grateful acknowledgments for the many important suggestions which he received from them, during the progress of its preparation.

Having said thus much, he would simply add, that, TO THE LOVERS OF TRUTH, THE WORK IS NOW RESPECTFULLY DEDICATED, WITH THE KIND

REGARDS OF

THE AUTHOR.

CHAPTER I.

INTRODUCTORY OBSERVATIONS.

IMPORTANCE OF THE SUBJECT.

THE doctrine of the Will is a cardinal doctrine of theology, as well as of mental philosophy. This doctrine, to say the least, is one of the great central points, from which the various different and conflicting systems of theological, mental, and moral science, take their departure. To determine a man's sentiments in respect to the Will, is to determine his position, in most important respects, as a theologian, and mental and moral philosopher. If we turn our thoughts inward, for the purpose of knowing what we are, what we ought to do, and to be, and what we shall become, as the result of being and doing what we ought or ought not, this doctrine presents itself at once, as one of the great pivots on which the resolution of all these questions turns.

If, on the other hand, we turn our thoughts from ourselves, to a study of the character of God, and of the nature and character of the government which He exercises over rational beings, all our apprehensions here, all our notions in respect to the nature and desert of sin and holiness, will, in many fundamental particulars, be determined by our notions in respect to the Will. In other words, our apprehensions of the nature and character of the Divine government, must be determined, in most important respects, by our conceptions of the nature and powers of the subjects of that government. I have no wish to conceal from the reader the true bearing of our present inquiries. I wish him distinctly to understand, that in fixing his notions in respect to the doctrine of the Will, he is determining a point of observation from which, and a medium through which, he shall contemplate his own character and deserts as a moral agent, and the nature and character of that Divine government, under which he must ever "live, and move, and have his being."

TRUE AND FALSE METHODS OF INQUIRY.

Such being the bearing of our present inquiries, an important question arises, to wit: What should be the influence of such considerations upon our investigations in this department of mental science It should not surely induce us, as appears to be true in the case of many divines and philosophers even, first to form our system of theology, and then, in the light of that, to determine our theory of the Will. The true science of the Will, as well as that of all ether departments of mental philosophy, "does not come by observation," but by internal reflection. Because our doctrine of the Will, whether true or false, will have a controlling influence in determining the character of our theology, and the meaning which we shall attach to large portions of the Bible, that doctrine does not, for that reason, lose its exclusively psychological character. Every legitimate question pertaining to it, still remains purely and exclusively a psychological question. The mind has but one eye by which it can see itself, and that is the eye of consciousness. This, then, is the organ of vision to be exclusively employed in all our inquiries in every department of mental science, and in none more exclusively than in that of the Will. We know very well, for example, that the science of optics has a fundamental bearing upon that of Astronomy. What if a philosopher, for that reason, should form his theory of optics by looking at the stars? This would be perfectly analogous to the conduct of a divine or philosopher who should determine his theory of the Will, not by psychological reflection, but by a system of theology formed without such reflection. Suppose again, that the science of Geometry had the same influence in theology, that that of the Will now has. This fact would not change at all the nature of that science, nor the mode proper in conducting our investigations in respect to it. It would still remain a science of demonstration, with all its principles and rules of investigation unchanged. So with the doctrine of the Will. Whatever its bearings upon other sciences may be, it still remains no less exclusively a psychological science. It has its own principles and laws of investigation, principles and laws as independent of systems of theology, as the principles and laws of the science of optics are of those of Astronomy. In pursuing our investigations in all other departments of mental science, we, for the time being, cease to be theologians. We become mental philosophers. Why should the study of the Will be an exception?

The question now returns--what should be the bearing of the fact, that our theory of the Will, whether right or wrong, will have an important influence in determining our system of theology? This surely should be its influence. It should induce in us great care and caution in our investigations in this department of mental science. We are laying the foundation of the most important edifice of which it ever entered into the heart of man to conceive--

an edifice, all the parts, dimensions, and proportions of which, we are required most sedulously to conform to the "pattern shown us in the mount." Under such circumstances, who should not be admonished, that he should "dig deep, and lay his foundation upon a rock?" I will therefore, in view of what has been said above, earnestly bespeak four things of the reader of the following treatise.

1. That he read it as an honest, earnest inquirer after truth.

2. That he give that degree of attention to the work, that is requisite to an understanding of it.

3. That when he dissents from any of its fundamental principles, he will distinctly state to his own mind the reason and ground of that dissent, and carefully investigate its validity. If these principles are wrong, such an investigation will render the truth more conspicuous to the mind, confirm the mind in the truth, and furnish it with means to overturn the opposite error.

4. That he pursue his investigations with implicit confidence in the distinct affirmations of his own consciousness in respect to this subject. Such a suggestion would appear truly singular, if made in respect to any other department of mental science but that of the Will. Here it is imperiously called for so long have philosophers and divines been accustomed to look without, to determine the characteristics of phenomena which appear exclusively within, and which are revealed to the eye of consciousness only. Having been so long under the influence of this pernicious habit, it will require somewhat of an effort for the mind to turn its organ of self-vision in upon itself, for the purpose of correctly reporting to itself, what is really passing in that inner sanctuary. Especially will it require an effort to do this, with a fixed determination to abandon all theories formed from external observation, and to follow implicitly the results of observations made internally. This method we must adopt, however, or there is at once an end of all real science, not only in respect to the Will, but to all other departments of the mind. Suppose an individual to commence a treatise on colors, for example, with a denial of the validity of all affirmations of the Intelligence through the eye, in respect to the phenomena about which he is to treat. What would be thought of such a treatise? The moment we deny the validity of the affirmations of any of our faculties, in respect to the appropriate

objects of those faculties, all reasoning about those objects becomes the height of absurdity. So in respect to the mind. If we doubt or deny the validity of the affirmations of consciousness in respect to the nature and characteristics of all mental operations, mental philosophy becomes impossible, and all reasoning in respect to the mind perfectly absurd. Implicit confidence in the distinct affirmations of consciousness, is a fundamental law of all correct philosophizing in every department of mental science. Permit me most earnestly to bespeak this confidence, as we pursue our investigations in respect to the Will.

COMMON FAULT.

It may be important here to notice a common fault in the method frequently adopted by philosophers in their investigations in this department of mental science. In the most celebrated treatise that has ever appeared upon this subject, the writer does not recollect to have met with a single appeal to consciousness, the only adequate witness in the case. The whole treatise, almost, consists of a series of syllogisms, linked together with apparent perfectness, syllogisms pertaining to an abstract something called Will. Throughout the whole, the facts of consciousness are never appealed to. In fact, in instances not a few, among writers of the same school, the right to make such an appeal, on the ground of the total inadequacy of consciousness to give testimony in the case, has been formally denied. Would it be at all strange, if it should turn out that all the fundamental results of investigations conducted after such a method, should be wholly inapplicable to the Will, the phenomena of which lie under the eye of consciousness, or to stand in plain contradiction to the phenomena thus affirmed? What, from the method adopted, we see is very likely to take place, we find, from experience, to be actually true of the treatise above referred to. This is noticed by the distinguished author of The Natural History of Enthusiasm, in an Essay introductory to Edwards on the Will. "Even the reader," he says, "who is scarcely at all familiar with abstruse science, will, if he follow our author attentively, be perpetually conscious of a vague dissatisfaction, or latent suspicion, that some fallacy has passed into the train of propositions, although the linking of syllogisms seems perfect. This suspicion will increase in strength as he proceeds, and will at length condense itself into the form of a protest against certain conclusions, notwithstanding their apparently necessary connection with the premises." What should we expect from a treatise on mental science, from which the affirmations of consciousness should be formally excluded, as grounds of any important conclusions? Just what we find to be true, in fact, of the above named treatise on the Will; to wit: all its fundamental conclusions positively contradicted by such affirmations. What if the decisions of our courts of justice were based upon data from which the testimony of all material witnesses has been formally excluded? Who would look to such decisions as the exponents of truth and justice? Yet all the elements in those decisions may be the necessary logical consequents of the data actually assumed. Such decisions may be all wrong, however, from the fact that the data which ought to be assumed in the case, were excluded. The same will, almost of necessity, be true of all treatises, in every department of mental science, which are not based upon the facts of consciousness.

PROPER METHOD OF REASONING FROM REVELATION TO THE SYSTEM OF MENTAL PHILOSOPHY THEREIN PRE-SUPPOSED.

By what has been said, the reader will not understand me as denying the propriety of comparing our conclusions in mental science with the Bible. Though no system of mental philosophy is directly revealed in the Bible, some one system is therein pre-supposed, and assuming, as we do, that the Scriptures are a revelation from God, we must suppose that the system of mental science assumed in the sacred writings, is the true system. If we could find the system pre-supposed in the Bible, we should have an infallible standard by which to test the validity of any conclusions to which we have arrived, as the results of psychological investigation. It is therefore a very legitimate, interesting, and profitable inquiry--what is the system of mental science assumed as true in the Bible? We may very properly turn our attention to the solution of such a question. In doing this, however, two things should be kept distinctly in mind.

1. In such inquiries, we leave the domain of mental philosophy entirely, and enter that of theology. In the latter we are to be guided by principles entirely distinct from those demanded in the former.

2. In reasoning from the Bible to the system of mental philosophy pre-supposed in the Scriptures, we are in danger of assuming wrong data as the basis of our conclusions that is, we are in danger of drawing our inferences

from those truths of Scripture which have no legitimate bearing upon the subject, and of overlooking those which do have such a bearing. While there are truths of inspiration from which we may properly reason to the theory of the Will, pre-supposed in the Bible, there are other truths from which we cannot legitimately thus reason. Now suppose that we have drawn our conclusions from truths of inspiration which have no legitimate bearing upon the subject, truths which, if we do reason from them in the case, will lead us to wrong conclusions; suppose that in the light of such conclusions we have explained the facts of consciousness, assuming that such must be their true character, else we deny the Bible. Shall we not then have almost inextricably lost ourselves in the labyrinth of error?

The following principles may be laid down as universally binding, if we would reason correctly, as philosophers and theologians, on the subject under consideration.

1. In the domain of philosophy, we must confine ourselves strictly and exclusively to the laws of psychological investigation, without reference to any system of theology.

2. In the domain of theology, when we would reason from the truths of inspiration to the theory of the Will pre-supposed in the Bible, we should be exceedingly careful to reason from those truths only which have a direct and decisive bearing upon the subject, and not from those which have no such bearing.

3. We should carefully compare the conclusions to which we have arrived in each of these domains, assuming that if they do not harmonize, we have erred either as philosophers or theologians.

4. In case of disagreement, we should renew our independent investigations in each domain, for the purpose of detecting the error into which we have fallen.

In conducting an investigation upon such principles, we shall, with almost absolute certainty, find ourselves in each domain, following rays of light, which will converge together in the true theory of the Will.

ERRORS OF METHOD.

Two errors into which philosophers and divines of a certain class have fallen in their method of treating the department of our subject now under consideration, here demand a passing notice.

1. The two methods above referred to, the psychological and theological, which should at all times be kept entirely distinct and separate, have unhappily been mingled together. Thus the subject has failed to receive a proper investigation in the domain, either of theology or of philosophy.

2. In reasoning from the Scriptures to the theory of the Will pre-supposed in the same, the wrong truth has been adduced as the basis of such reasoning, to wit: the fact of the Divine foreknowledge. As all events yet future are foreknown to God, they are in themselves, it is said, alike certain. This certainty necessitates the adoption of a particular theory of the Will. Now before we can draw any such conclusion from the truth before us, the following things pertaining to it we need to know with absolute certainty, things which God has not revealed, and which we never can know, until He has revealed them, to wit: the mode, the nature, and the degree of the Divine foreknowledge. Suppose that God should impart to us apprehensions perfectly full and distinct, of the mode, nature and degree of His foreknowledge of human conduct. How do we know but that we should then see with the most perfect clearness, that this foreknowledge is just as consistent with the theory of the Will, denied by the philosophers and divines under consideration, as with that which they suppose necessarily to result from the Divine foreknowledge? This, then, is not the truth from which we should reason to the theory of the Will pre-supposed in the Bible.

There are truths of inspiration, however, which appear to me to have a direct and decisive bearing upon this subject, and upon which we may therefore safely base our conclusions. In the Scriptures, man is addressed as a moral agent, the subject of commands and prohibitions, of obligation, of merit and demerit, and consequently of reward and punishment. Now when we have determined the powers which an agent must possess, to render him a proper subject of command and prohibition, of obligation, of merit and demerit, and consequently of reward and punishment, we have determined the philosophy of the Will, really pre-supposed in the Scriptures. Beneath these truths, therefore, and not beneath that of the divine foreknowledge, that philosophy is to be sought for. This I argue--

1. Because the former has a direct, while the latter has only an indirect bearing upon the subject.

2. Of the former our ideas are perfectly clear and distinct, while of the mode, the degree, and the nature of the Divine foreknowledge we are profoundly ignorant. To all eternity, our ideas of the nature of commands and prohibitions, of obligations, of merit and demerit, and of reward and punishment grounded on moral desert, can never be more clear and distinct than they now are. From such truths, then, and not from those that we do not understand, and which at the utmost have only an indirect bearing upon the subject, we ought to reason, if we reason at all, to the philosophy of the Will pre-supposed in the Scriptures. The reader is now put in possession of the method that will be pursued in the following treatise, and is consequently prepared to enter upon the investigation of the subject before us.

CHAPTER II.

CLASSIFICATION OF THE MENTAL FACULTIES.

EVERY individual who has reflected with any degree of interest upon the operations of his own mind, cannot have failed to notice three classes of mental phenomena, each of which is entirely distinct from either of the others. These phenomena, which comprehend the entire operations of the mind, and which may be expressed by the terms thinking, feeling, and willing, clearly indicate in the mind three faculties equally distinct from one another. These faculties are denominated the Intellect, the Sensibility or Sensitivity, and the Will. To the first, all intellectual operations, such as perceiving, thinking, judging, knowing, &c., are referred. To the second, we refer all sensitive states, all feelings, such as sensations, emotions, desires, &c. To the Will, or the active voluntary faculty, are referred all mental determinations, such as purposes, intentions, resolutions, choices and volitions.

CLASSIFICATION VERIFIED.

1. The classes of phenomena, by which this tri-unity of the mental powers is

indicated, differ from one another, not in degree, but in kind. Thought, whether clear or obscure, in all degrees, remains equally distinct, in its nature, from feelings and determinations of every class. So of feelings. Sensations, emotions, desires, all the phenomena of the Sensibility, in all degrees and modifications, remain, in their nature and essential characteristics, equally distinct from thought on the one hand, and the action of the Will on the other. The same holds true of the phenomena of the Will. A resolution, for example, in one degree, is not a thought in another, a sensation, emotion, or desire and in another a choice, purpose, intention, or volition. In all degrees and modifications, the phenomena of the Will, in their nature and essential characteristics, remain equally distinct from the operations of the Intelligence on the one hand, and of the Sensibility on the other.

2. This distinction is recognized by universal consciousness. When, for example, one speaks of thinking of any particular object, then of desiring it, and subsequently of determining to obtain the object, for the purpose of gratifying that desire, all mankind most clearly recognize his meaning in each of the above-named affirmations, and understand him as speaking of three entirely distinct classes of mental operations. No person, under such circumstances, ever confounds one of these states with either of the others. So clearly marked and distinguished is the three-fold classification of mental phenomena under consideration, in the spontaneous affirmations of universal consciousness.

3. In all languages, also, there are distinct terms appropriated to the expression of these three classes of phenomena, and of the mental power indicated by the same. In the English language, for example, we have the terms thinking, feeling, and willing, each of which is applied to one particular class of these mental phenomena, and never to either of the others. We have also the terms Intellect, Sensibility, and Will, appropriated, in a similar manner, to designate the mental powers indicated by these phenomena. In all other languages, especially among nations of any considerable advancement in mental culture, we find terms of precisely similar designation. What do such facts indicate? They clearly show, that in the development of the universal Intelligence, the different classes of phenomena under consideration have been distinctly marked, and distinguished from one another, together with the three-fold division of the mental powers indicated by the same phenomena.

4. The clearness and particularity with which the universal intelligence has marked the distinction under consideration, is strikingly indicated by the fact, that there are qualifying terms in common use which are applied to each of these classes of phenomena, and never to either of the others. It is true that there are such terms which are promiscuously applied to all classes of mental phenomena. There are terms, however, which are never applied to but one class. Thus we speak of clear thoughts, but never of clear feelings or determinations. We speak of irrepressible feelings and desires, but never of irrepressible thoughts or resolutions. We also speak of inflexible determinations, but never of inflexible feelings or conceptions. With what perfect distinctness, then, must universal consciousness have marked thoughts, feelings, and determinations of the Will, as phenomena entirely distinct from one another--phenomena differing not in degree, but in kind, and as most clearly indicating the three-fold division of the mental powers under consideration.

5. So familiar are mankind with this distinction, so distinctly marked is it in their minds, that in familiar intercourse, when no particular theory of the mental powers is in contemplation, they are accustomed to speak of the Intellect, Sensibility, and Will, and of their respective phenomena, as entirely distinct from one another. Take a single example from Scripture. "What I shall choose, I wot not--having a desire to depart." Here the Apostle evidently speaks of desire and choice as phenomena differing in kind, and not in degree. "If you engage his heart" [his feelings], says Lord Chesterfield, speaking of a foreign minister, "you have a fair chance of imposing upon his understanding, and determining his Will." "His Will," says another writer, speaking of the insane, "is no longer restrained by his Judgment, but driven madly on by his passions."

"When wit is overruled by Will, And Will is led by fond Desire, Then Reason may as well be still, As speaking, kindle greater fire."[1]

In all the above extracts the tri-unity of the mental powers, as consisting of the Intellect, Sensibility, and Will, is distinctly recognized. Yet the writers had, at the time, no particular theory of mental philosophy in contemplation. They speak of a distinction of the mental faculties which all understand and recognize as real, as soon as suggested to their minds.

The above considerations are abundantly sufficient to verify the three-fold distinction above made, of mental phenomena and powers. Two suggestions arise here which demand special attention.

1. To confound either of these distinct powers of the mind with either of the others, as has been done by several philosophers of eminence, in respect to the Will and Sensibility, is a capital error in mental science. If one faculty is confounded with another, the fundamental characteristics of the former will of course be confounded with the same characteristics of the latter. Thus the worst forms of error will be introduced not only into philosophy, but theology, too, as far as the latter science is influenced by the former. What would be thought of a treatise on mental science, in which the Will should be confounded with the Intelligence, and in which thinking and willing would be consequently represented as phenomena identical in kind? This would be an error no more capital, no more glaring, no more distinctly contradicted by fundamental phenomena, than the confounding of the Will with the Sensibility.

2. We are now prepared to contemplate one of the great errors of Edwards in his immortal work on the Will--an error which we meet with in the commencement of that work, and which lays a broad foundation for the false conclusions subsequently found in it. He has confounded the Will with the Sensibility. Of course, we should expect to find that he has subsequently confounded the fundamental characteristics of the phenomena of the former faculty, with the same characteristics of the latter.

"God has endowed the soul," he says, "with two faculties: One is that by which it is capable of perception and speculation, or by which it discerns, and views, and judges of things; which is called the understanding. The other faculty is that by which the soul does not merely perceive and view things, but is some way inclined to them, or is disinclined and averse from them; or is the faculty by which the soul does not behold things as an indifferent, unaffected spectator; but either as liking or disliking, pleased or displeased, approving or rejecting. This faculty, as it has respect to the actions that are determined by it, is called the Will."

From his work on the Affections, I cite the following to the same import:

"The Affections of the soul," he observes, "are not properly distinguished from the Will, as though they were two faculties of the soul. All acts of the Affections of the soul are, in some sense, acts of the Will, and all acts of the Will are acts of the affections. All exercises of the Will are, in some degree or other, exercises of the soul's appetition or aversion; or which is the same thing, of its love or hatred. The soul wills one thing rather than another, or chooses one thing rather than another, no otherwise than as it loves one thing more than another." "The Affections are only certain modes of the exercise of the Will." "The Affections are no other than the more vigorous and sensible exercises of the inclination and will of the soul."

Whether he has or has not subsequently confounded the fundamental characteristics of the phenomena of the Will with those of the phenomena of the Sensibility will be seen in the progress of the present treatise.

CHAPTER III.

LIBERTY AND NECESSITY.

WE come now to consider the great and fundamental characteristic of the Will, that by which it is, in a special sense, distinguished from each of the other mental faculties, to wit: that of Liberty.

SEC. I. TERMS DEFINED.

Our first inquiry respects the meaning of the term Liberty as distinguished from that of Necessity. These terms do not differ, as expressing genus and species; that is, Liberty does not designate a species of which Necessity expresses the genus. On the other hand, they differ by way of opposition. All correct definitions of terms thus related, will possess these two characteristics. 1. They will mutually exclude each other that is, what is affirmed of one, will, in reality, be denied of the other. 2. They will be so defined as to be universal in their application. The terms right and wrong, for example, thus differ from each other. In the light of all correct definitions of these terms, it will be seen with perfect distinctness, 1st, that to affirm of an action that it is right, is equivalent to an affirmation that it is not wrong; and to affirm that it is wrong, is to affirm that it is not right; 2d, that all moral actions, actual and conceivable, must be either right or wrong. So of all other terms thus related.

The meaning of the terms Liberty and Necessity, as distinguished the one from the other, may be designated by a reference to two relations perfectly distinct and opposite, which may be supposed to exist between an antecedent and its consequent.

1. The antecedent being given, one, and only one, consequent can possibly arise, and that consequent must arise. This relation we designate by the term Necessity. I place my finger, for example, constituted as my physical system now is, in the flame of a burning candle, and hold it there for a given time. The two substances in contact is the antecedent. The feeling of intense pain which succeeds is the consequent. Now such is universally believed to be the correlation between the nature of these substances, that under the circumstances supposed, but one consequent can possibly arise, and that consequent must arise; to wit--the feeling of pain referred to. The relation between such an antecedent and its consequent, therefore, we, in all instances, designate by the term Necessity. When the relation of Necessity is pre-supposed, in the presence of a new consequent, we affirm absolutely that of a new antecedent.

2. The second relation is this. The antecedent being given, either of two or more consequents is equally possible, and therefore, when one consequent does arise, we affirm that either of the others might have arisen in its stead. When this relation is pre-supposed, from the appearance of a new consequent, we do not necessarily affirm the presence of a new antecedent. This relation we designate by the term Liberty.

CHARACTERISTICS OF THE ABOVE DEFINITIONS.

On the above definitions I remark:

1. That they mutually exclude each other. To predicate Liberty of any phenomenon is to affirm that it is not necessary. To predicate Necessity of it, is equivalent to an affirmation that it is not free.

2. They are strictly and absolutely universal in their application. All

antecedents and consequents, whatever the nature of the subjects thus connected may be, must fall under one or the other of these relations. As the terms right and wrong, when correctly defined, will express the nature of all moral actions, actual and conceivable, so the terms Liberty and Necessity, as above defined, clearly indicate the nature of the relation between all antecedents and consequents, real and supposable. Take any antecedent and consequent we please, real or conceivable, and we know absolutely, that they must sustain to each other one or the other of these relations. Either in connection with this antecedent, but this one consequent is possible, and this must arise, or in connection with the same antecedent, either this, or one or more different consequents are possible, and consequently equally so: for possibility has, in reality, no degrees.

3. All the phenomena of the Will, sustaining, as they do, the relation of consequents to motives considered as antecedents, must fall under one or the other of these relations. If we say, that the relation between motives and acts of Will is that of certainty, still this certainty must arise from a necessary relation between the antecedent and its consequent, or it must be of such a nature as consists with the relation of Liberty, in the sense of the term Liberty as above defined.

4. The above definitions have this great advantage in our present investigations. They at once free the subject from the obscurity and perplexity in which it is often involved by the definitions of philosophers. They are accustomed, in many instances, to speak of moral necessity and physical necessity, as if these are in reality different kinds of necessity: whereas the terms moral and physical, in such connections, express the nature of the subjects sustaining to each other the relations of antecedents and consequents, and not at all that of the relation existing between them. This is exclusively expressed by the term Necessity--a term which designates a relation which is always one and the same, whatever the nature of the subjects thus related may be. An individual in a treatise on natural science, might, if he should choose, in speaking of the relations of antecedents and consequents among solid, fluid, and aeriform substances, use the words, solid necessity, fluid necessity, and aeriform necessity. He might use as many qualifying terms as there are different subjects sustaining to each other the relation under consideration. In all such instances no error will arise, if these qualifying terms are distinctly understood to designate, not the nature of the

relation of antecedent and consequent in any given case (as if there were as many different kinds of necessity as there are qualifying terms used), but to designate the nature of the subjects sustaining this relation. If, on the other hand, the impression should be made, that each of these qualifying terms designates a necessity of a peculiar kind, and if, as a consequence, the belief should be induced, that there are in reality so many different kinds of necessity, errors of the gravest character would arise--errors no more important, however, than actually do arise from the impression often induced, that moral necessity differs in kind from physical necessity.

5. I mention another very decisive advantage which the above definitions have in our present investigations. In the light of the terms Liberty and Necessity, as above defined, the two great schools in philosophy and theology are obliged to join issue directly upon the real question in difference between them, without the possibility on the part of either, of escaping under a fog of definitions about moral necessity, physical necessity, moral certainty, &c., and then claiming a victory over their opponents. These terms, as above defined, stand out with perfect clearness and distinctness to all reflecting minds. Every one must see, that the phenomena of the Will cannot but fall under the one or the other of the relations designated by these terms inasmuch as no third relation differing in kind from both of these, is conceivable. The question therefore may be fairly put to every individual, without the possibility of misapprehension or evasion--Do you believe, whenever a man puts forth an act of Will, that in those circumstances, this one act only is possible, and that this act cannot but arise? In all prohibited acts, for example, do you believe that an individual, by the resistless providence of God, is placed in circumstances in which this one act only is possible, and this cannot but result, that in these identical circumstances, another and a different act is required of him, and that for not putting forth this last act, he is justly held as infinitely guilty in the sight of God, and of the moral universe? To these questions every one must give an affirmative or negative answer. If he gives the former, he holds the doctrine of Necessity, and must take that doctrine with all its consequences. If he gives the latter, he holds the doctrine of Liberty in the sense of the term as above defined. He must hold, that in the identical circumstances in which a given act of Will is put forth, another and different act might have been put forth; and that for this reason, in all prohibited acts, a moral agent is held justly responsible for different and opposite acts. Much is gained to the cause of truth, when, as in

the present instance, the different schools are obliged to join issue directly upon the real question in difference between them, and that without the possibility of misapprehension or evasion in respect to the nature of that question.

MOTIVE DEFINED.

Having settled the meaning of the terms Liberty and Necessity, as designating two distinct and opposite relations, the only relations conceivable between an antecedent and its consequent, one other term which may not unfrequently be used in the following treatise, remains to be defined; to wit-- motive--a term which designates that which sustains to the phenomena of the Will, the relation of antecedent. Volition, choice, preference, intention, all the phenomena of the Will, are considered as the consequent. Whatever within the mind itself may be supposed to influence its determinations, whether called susceptibilities, biases, or anything else; and all influences acting upon it as incentives from without, are regarded as the antecedent. I use the term motive as synonymous with antecedent as above defined. It designates all the circumstances and influences from within or without the mind, which operate upon it to produce any given act of Will.

The term antecedent in the case before us, in strictness of speech, has this difference of meaning from that of motive as above defined: The former includes all that is designated by the latter, together with the Will itself. No difficulty or obscurity, however, will result from the use of these terms as synonymous, in the sense explained.

SEC. II. LIBERTY, AS OPPOSED TO NECESSITY, THE CHARACTERISTIC OF THE WILL.

We are now prepared to meet the question, To which of the relations above defined shall we refer the phenomena of the Will? If these phenomena are subject to the law of necessity, then, whenever a particular antecedent (motive) is given, but one consequent (act of Will) is possible, and that consequent must arise. It cannot possibly but take place. If, on the other hand, these phenomena fall under the relation of Liberty, whenever any particular motive is present, either of two or more acts of Will is equally possible; and when any particular consequent (act of Will) does arise, either of the other consequents might have arisen in its stead.

Before proceeding directly to argue the question before us, one consideration of a general nature demands a passing notice. It is this. The simple statement of the question, in the light of the above relations, settles it, and must settle it, in the judgment of all candid, uncommitted inquirers after the truth. Let any individual contemplate the action of his voluntary powers in the light of the relations of Liberty and Necessity as above defined, and he will spontaneously affirm the fact, that he is a free and not a necessary agent, and affirm it as absolutely as he affirms his own existence. Wherever he is, while he retains the consciousness of rational being, this conviction will and must be to him an omnipresent reality. To escape it, he must transcend the bounds of conscious existence.

OBJECTIONS TO THE DOCTRINE OF NECESSITY.

Such is the importance of the subject, however, that a more extended and particular consideration of it is demanded. In the further prosecution of the argument upon the subject, we will--

I. In the first place, contemplate the position, that the phenomena of the Will are subject to the laws of Necessity. In taking this position we are at once met with the following palpable and insuperable difficulties.

1. The conviction above referred to--a conviction which remains proof against all apparent demonstrations to the contrary. We may pile demonstration upon demonstration in favor of the doctrine of Necessity, still, as the mind falls back upon the spontaneous affirmations of its own Intelligence, it finds, in the depths of its inner being, a higher demonstration of the fact, that that doctrine is and must be false--that man is not the agent which that doctrine affirms him to be. In the passage already cited, and which I will take occasion here to repeat, the writer has, with singular correctness, mapped out the unvarying experience of the readers of Edwards on the Will. "Even the reader," he says, "who is scarcely at all familiar with abstruse science, will, if he follow our author attentively, be perpetually conscious of a vague dissatisfaction, or latent suspicion, that some fallacy has passed into the train of propositions, although the linking of syllogisms seems perfect. This suspicion will increase in strength as he proceeds, and will at length

condense itself into the form of a protest against certain conclusions, notwithstanding their apparently necessary connection with the premises." What higher evidence can we have that that treatise gives a false interpretation of the facts of universal consciousness pertaining to the Will, than is here presented? Any theory which gives a distinct and true explanation of the facts of consciousness, will be met by the Intelligence with the response, "That's true; I have found it." Any theory apparently supported by adequate evidence, but which still gives a false interpretation of such facts, will induce the internal conflict above described--a conflict which, as the force of apparent demonstration increases, will, in the very centre of the Intelligence, "condense itself into the form of a protest against the conclusions presented, notwithstanding their apparently necessary connection with the premises." The falsity of the doctrine of Necessity is a first truth of the universal Intelligence.

2. If this doctrine is true, it is demonstrably evident, that in no instance, real or supposable, have men any power whatever to will or to act differently from what they do. The connection between the determinations of the Will, and their consequents, external and internal, is absolutely necessary. Constituted as I now am, if I will, for example, a particular motion of my hand or arm, no other movement, in these circumstances, was possible, and this movement could not but take place. The same holds true of all consequents, external and internal, of all acts of Will. Let us now suppose that these acts themselves are the necessary consequents of the circumstances in which they originate. In what conceivable sense have men, in the circumstances in which Providence places them, power either to will or to act differently from what they do? The doctrine of ability to will or to do differently from what we do is, in every sense, false, if the doctrine of Necessity is true. Men, when they transgress the moral law, always sin, without the possibility of doing right. From this position the Necessitarian cannot escape.

3. On this theory, God only is responsible for all human volitions together with their effects. The relation between all antecedents and their consequents was established by him. If that relation be in all instances a necessary one, his Will surely is the sole responsible antecedent of all consequents.

4. The idea of obligation, of merit and demerit, and of the consequent

propriety of reward and punishment, are chimeras. To conceive of a being deserving praise or blame, for volitions or actions which occurred under circumstances in which none others were possible, and in which these could not possibly but happen, is an absolute impossibility. To conceive him under obligation to have given existence, under such circumstances, to different consequents, is equally impossible. It is to suppose an agent under obligation to perform that to which Omnipotence is inadequate. For Omnipotence cannot perform impossibilities. It cannot reverse the law of Necessity. Let any individual conceive of creatures placed by Divine Providence in circumstances in which but one act, or series of acts of Will, can arise, and these cannot but arise--let him, then, attempt to conceive of these creatures as under obligation, in these same circumstances, to give existence to different and opposite acts, and as deserving of punishment for not doing so. He will find it as impossible to pass such a judgment as to conceive of the annihilation of space, or of an event without a cause. To conceive of necessity and obligation as fundamental elements of the same act, is an absolute impossibility. The human Intelligence is incapable of affirming such contradictions.

5. As an additional consideration, to show the absolute incompatibility of the idea of moral obligation with the doctrine of Necessity, permit me to direct the attention of the reader to this striking fact. While no man, holding the doctrine of Liberty as above defined, was ever known to deny moral obligation, such denial has, without exception, in every age and nation, been avowedly based upon the assumption of the truth of the doctrine of Necessity. In every age and nation, in every solitary mind in which the idea of obligation has been denied, this doctrine has been the great maelstrom in which this idea has been swallowed up and lost. How can the Necessitarian account for such facts in consistency with his theory?

6. The commands of God addressed to men as sinners and requiring them in all cases of transgression of the moral law, to choose and to act differently from what they do, are, if this doctrine is true, the perfection of tyranny. In all such cases men are required--

(1.) To perform absolute impossibilities; to reverse the law of necessity.

(2.) To do that to which Omnipotence is inadequate. For Omnipotence, as we have seen, cannot reverse the law of necessity. Not only so, but--

(3.) Men in all such instances are required, as a matter of fact, to resist and overcome Omnipotence. To require us to reverse the relation established by Omnipotence, between antecedents and consequents, is certainly to require us to resist and overcome Omnipotence, and that in the absence of all power, even to attempt the accomplishment of that which we are required to accomplish.

7. If this doctrine is true, at the final Judgment the conscience and intelligence of the universe will and must be on the side of the condemned. Suppose that when the conduct of the wicked shall be revealed at that Day, another fact shall stand out with equal conspicuousness, to wit, that God himself had placed these beings where but one course of conduct was possible to them, and that course they could not but pursue, to wit, the course which they did pursue, and that for having pursued this course, the only one possible, they are now to be "punished with everlasting destruction from the presence of God and the glory of his power," must not the intelligence of the universe pronounce such a sentence unjust? All this must be true, or the doctrine of Necessity is false. Who can believe, that the pillars of God's eternal government rest upon such a doctrine?

8. On this supposition, probation is an infinite absurdity. We might with the same propriety represent the specimens in the laboratory of the chemist, as on probation, as men, if their actions are the necessary result of the circumstances in which Omnipotence has placed them. What must intelligent beings think of probation for a state of eternal retribution, probation based on such a principle?

9. The doctrine of Necessity is, in all essential particulars, identical with Fatalism in its worst form. All that Fatalism ever has maintained, or now maintains, is, that men, by a power which they cannot control nor resist, are placed in circumstances in which they cannot but pursue the course of conduct which they actually are pursuing. This doctrine has never affirmed, that, in the Necessitarian sense, men cannot "do as they please." All that it maintains is, that they cannot but please to do as they do. Thus this doctrine differs not one "jot or tittle," from Necessity. No man can show the want of perfect identity between them. Fatalists and Necessitarians may differ in regard to the origin of this Necessity. In regard to its nature, the only thing

material, as far as present inquiries are concerned, they do not differ at all.

10. In maintaining the Necessity of all acts of the Will of man, we must maintain, that the Will of God is subject to the same law. This is universally admitted by Necessitarians themselves. Now in maintaining the necessity of all acts of the Divine Will, the following conclusions force themselves upon us:

(1.) MOTIVES which necessitate the determinations of the Divine Will, are the sole originating and efficient causes in existence. God is not the first cause of anything.

(2.) To motives, which of course exist independently of the Divine Will, we must ascribe the origin of all created existences. The glory of originating "all things visible and invisible," belongs not to Him, but to motives.

(3.) In all cases in which creatures are required to act differently from what they do, as in all acts of sin, they are in reality required not only to resist and overcome the omnipotent determinations of the Divine Will, but also the motives by which the action of God's Will is necessitated. We ask Necessitarians to look these consequences in the face, and then say, whether they are prepared to deny, or to meet them.

11. Finally, if the doctrine under consideration is true, in all instances of the transgression of the moral law, men are, in reality, required to produce an event which, when it does exist, shall exist without a cause. In circumstances where but one event is possible, and that cannot but arise, if a different event should arise, it would undeniably be an event without a cause. To require such an event under such circumstances, is to require an event without a cause, the most palpable contradiction conceivable. Now just such a requirement as this is laid upon men, in all cases of disobedience of the moral law, if the doctrine of Necessity is true. In all such cases, according to this doctrine men are placed in circumstances in which but one act is possible, and that must arise, to wit: the act of disobedience which is put forth. If, in these circumstances, an act of obedience should be put forth, it would be an event without a cause, and in opposition also to the action of a necessary cause. In these identical circumstances, the act of obedience is required, that is, an act is required of creatures, which, if it should be put forth, would be an event without a cause. Has a God of truth and justice ever laid upon men

such a requisition as that? How, I ask, can the doctrine of Necessity be extricated from such a difficulty?

DOCTRINE OF LIBERTY--DIRECT ARGUMENT.

II. We will now, as a second general argument, consider the position, that the Will is subject in its determinations to the relation of Liberty, in opposition to that of Necessity. Here I would remark, that as the phenomena of the Will must fall under one or the other of these relations, and as it has been shown, that they cannot fall under that of Necessity, but one supposition remains. They must fall under that of Liberty, as opposed to Necessity. The intrinsic absurdity of supposing that a being, all of whose actions are necessary, is still accountable for such actions, is sufficient to overthrow the doctrine of Necessity for ever. A few additional considerations are deemed requisite, in order to present the evidence in favor of the Liberty of the Will.

1. The first that I present is this. As soon as the doctrine of Liberty, as above defined, is distinctly apprehended, it is spontaneously recognized by every mind, as the true, and only true exposition of the facts of its own consciousness pertaining to the phenomena of the Will. This doctrine is simply an announcement of the spontaneous affirmations of the universal Intelligence. This is the highest possible evidence of the truth of the doctrine.

2. The universal conviction of mankind, that their former course of conduct might have been different from what it was. I will venture to affirm, that there is not a person on earth, who has not this conviction resting upon his mind in respect to his own past life. It is important to analyze this conviction, in order to mark distinctly its bearing upon our present inquiries. This conviction is not the belief, that if our circumstances had been different, we might have acted differently from what we did. A man, for example, says to himself--"At such a time, and in such circumstances, I determined upon a particular course of conduct. I might have determined upon a different and opposite course. Why did I not?" These affirmations are not based upon the conviction, that, in different circumstances, we might have done differently. In all such affirmations we take into account nothing but the particular circumstances in which our determinations were formed. It is in view of these circumstances exclusively, that we affirm that our determinations might have

been different from what they were. Let the appeal be made to any individual whatever, whose mind is not at the time under the influence of any particular theory of the Will. You say, that at such a time, and under such circumstances, you determined upon a particular course, that you might then have resolved upon a different and opposite course, and that you blame yourself for not having done so. Is not this your real meaning? "If my circumstances had been different, I might have resolved upon a different course." No, he would reply. That is not my meaning. I was not thinking at all of a change of circumstances, when I made this affirmation. What I mean is, that in the circumstances in which I was, I might have done differently from what I did. This is the reason why I blame myself for not having done so. The same conviction, to wit: that without any change of circumstances our past course of life might have been different from what it was, rests upon every mind on earth in which the remembrance of the past dwells. Now this universal conviction is totally false, if the doctrine of Necessity is true. The doctrine of the Liberty of the Will must be true, or the universal Intelligence is a perpetual falsehood.

3. In favor of the doctrine of Liberty, I next appeal to the direct, deliberate, and universal testimony of consciousness. This testimony is given in three ways.

(1.) In the general conviction above referred to, that without any change of circumstances, our course of conduct might have been the opposite of what it was. Nothing but a universal consciousness of the Liberty of the Will, can account for this conviction.

(2.) Whenever any object of choice is submitted to the mind, consciousness affirms, directly and positively, that, under these identical circumstances, either of two or more acts of Will is equally possible. Every man in such circumstances is as conscious of such power as he is of his own existence. In confirmation of these affirmations, let any one make the appeal to his own consciousness, when about to put forth any act of Will. He will be just as conscious that either of two or more different determinations is, in the same circumstances, equally possible, as he is of any mental state whatever.

(3.) In reference to all deliberate determinations of Will in time past, the remembrance of them is attended with a consciousness the most positive, that, in the same identical circumstances, determinations precisely opposite might have been originated. Let any one recall any such determination, and the consciousness of a power to have determined differently will be just as distinctly recalled as the act itself. He cannot be more sure that he acted at all, than he will be, that he might have acted [determined] differently. All these affirmations of consciousness are false, if the doctrine of Liberty is not true.

4. A fundamental distinction which all mankind make between the phenomena of the Will, and those of the other faculties, the Sensibility for example, is a full confirmation of the doctrine of Liberty, as a truth of universal consciousness. A man is taken out of a burning furnace, with his physical system greatly injured by the fire. As a consequence, he subsequently experiences much suffering and inconvenience. For the injury done him by the fire, and for the pain subsequently experienced, he never blames or reproaches himself. With self-reproach he never says, Why, instead of being thus injured, did I not come out of the furnace as the three worthies did from that of Nebuchadnezzar? Why do I not now experience pleasure instead of pain, as a consequence of that injury? Suppose, now, that his fall into the furnace was the result of a determination formed for the purpose of self-murder. For that determination, and for not having, in the same circumstances, determined differently, he will ever after reproach himself, as most guilty in the sight of God and man. How shall we account for the absence of self-reproach in the former instance, and for its presence in the latter? If the appeal should be made to the subject, his answer would be ready. In respect to the injury and pain, in the circumstances supposed, they could not but be experienced. Such phenomena, therefore, can never be the occasion of self-reproach. In the condition in which the determination referred to was formed, a different and opposite resolution might have been originated. That particular determination, therefore, is the occasion of self-reproach. How shall we account for this distinction, which all mankind agree in making, between the phenomena of the Sensibility on the one hand, and of the Will on the other? But one supposition accounts for this fact, the universal consciousness, that the former are necessary, and the latter free that in the circumstances of their occurrence the former may not, and the latter may, be different from what they are.

5. On any other theory than that of Liberty, the words, obligation, merit and demerit, &c., are words without meaning. A man is, we will suppose, by Divine Providence, placed in circumstances in which he cannot possibly but

pursue one given course, or, which is the same thing, put forth given determinations. When it is said that, in these identical circumstances, he ought to pursue a different and opposite course, or to put forth different and opposite determinations, what conceivable meaning can we attach to the word ought, here? There is nothing, in the circumstances supposed, which the word, ought, or obligation, can represent. If we predicate merit or demerit of an individual thus circumstanced, we use words equally without meaning. Obligation and moral desert, in such a case, rest upon "airy nothing," without a "local habitation or a name."

On the other hand, if we suppose that the right and the wrong are at all times equally possible to an individual; that when he chooses the one, he might, in the same identical circumstances, choose the other; infinite meaning attaches to the words, ought, obligation, merit and demerit, when it is said that an individual thus circumstanced ought to do the right and avoid the wrong, and that he merits reward or punishment, when he does the one, or does not do the other. The ideas of obligation, merit and demerit, reward and punishment, and probation with reference to a state of moral retribution, are all chimeras, on any other supposition than that of the Liberty of the Will. With this doctrine, they all perfectly harmonize.

6. All moral government, all laws, human and Divine, have their basis in the doctrine of Liberty; and are the perfection of tyranny, on any other supposition. To place creatures in circumstances which necessitate a given course of conduct, and render every other course impossible, and then to require of them, under the heaviest sanctions, a different and opposite course--what can be tyranny if this is not?

OBJECTION IN BAR OF AN APPEAL TO CONSCIOUSNESS.

An objection which is brought by Necessitarians, in perpetual bar of an appeal to consciousness, to determine the fact whether the phenomena of the Will fall under the relation of Liberty or Necessity, here demands special attention. Consciousness, it is said, simply affirms, that, in given circumstances, we do, in fact, put forth certain acts of Will. But whether we can or cannot, in these circumstances, put forth other and opposite determinations, it does not and cannot make any affirmation at all. It does not, therefore, fall within the province of Consciousness to determine whether the phenomena of the Will are subject to the relation of Liberty or Necessity; and it is unphilosophical to appeal to that faculty to decide such a question. This objection, if valid, renders null and void much of what has been said upon this subject; and as it constitutes a stronghold of the Necessitarian, it becomes us to examine it with great care. In reply, I remark,

1. That if this objection holds in respect to the phenomena of the Will, it must hold equally in respect of those of the other faculties the Intelligence, for example. We will, therefore, bring the objection to a test, by applying it to certain intellectual phenomena. We will take, as an example, the universal and necessary affirmation, that "it is impossible for the same thing, at the same time, to be and not to be." Every one is conscious, in certain circumstances, of making this and other kindred affirmations. Now, if the objection under consideration is valid, all that we should be conscious of is the fact, that, under the circumstances supposed, we do, in reality, make particular affirmations; while, in reference to the question, whether, in the same circumstances, we can or cannot make different and opposite affirmations, we should have no consciousness at all. Now, I appeal to every man, whether, when he is conscious of making the affirmation, that it is impossible for the same thing, at the same time, to be and not to be, he is not equally conscious of the fact, that it is impossible for him to make the opposite affirmation whether, when he affirms that three and two make five, he is not conscious that it is impossible for him to affirm that three and two are six? In other words, when we are conscious of making certain intellectual affirmations, are we not equally conscious of an impossibility of making different and opposite affirmations? Every man is just as conscious of the fact, that the phenomena of his Intelligence fall under the relation of Necessity, as he is of making any affirmations at all. If this is not so, we cannot know but that it is possible for us to affirm and believe perceived contradictions. All that we could say is, that, as a matter of fact, we do not do it. But whether we can or cannot do it, we can never know. Do we not know, however, as absolutely as we know anything, that we cannot affirm perceived contradictions? In other words, we do and can know absolutely, that our Intelligence is subject to the law of Necessity. We do know by consciousness, with absolute certainty, that the phenomena of the Intelligence, and I may add, of the Sensibility too, do fall under the relation of Necessity. Why may we not know, with equal certainty, whether the phenomena of the Will do or do not fall under the relation of Liberty? What then becomes of the objection

under consideration?

2. But while we are conscious of the fact, that the Intellect is under the law of Necessity, we are equally conscious that Will is under that of Liberty. We make intellectual affirmations; such, for example, as the propositions, Things equal to the same things are equal to one another, There can be no event without a cause, &c., with a consciousness of an utter impossibility of making different and opposite affirmations. We put forth acts of Will with a consciousness equally distinct and absolute, of a possibility, in the same circumstances, of putting forth different and opposite determinations. Even Necessitarians admit and affirm the validity of the testimony of consciousness in the former instance. Why should we doubt or deny it in the latter?

3. The question, whether Consciousness can or cannot give us not only mental phenomena, but also the fundamental characteristics of such phenomena, cannot be determined by any pre-formed theory, in respect to what Consciousness can or cannot affirm. If we wish to know to what a witness is able to testify, we must not first determine what he can or cannot say, and then refuse to hear anything from him, except in conformity to such decisions. We must first give him a full and attentive hearing, and then judge of his capabilities. So in respect to Consciousness. If we wish to know what it does or does not, what it can or cannot affirm, we must let it give its full testimony, untrammelled by any pre-formed theories. Now, when the appeal is thus made, we find, that, in the circumstances in which we do originate given determinations, it affirms distinctly and absolutely, that, in the same identical circumstances, we might originate different and opposite determinations. From what Consciousness does affirm, we ought surely to determine the sphere of its legitimate affirmations.

4. The universal solicitude of Necessitarians to take the question under consideration from the bar of Consciousness is, in fact, a most decisive acknowledgment, on their part, that at that tribunal the cause will go against them. Let us suppose that all men were as conscious that their Will is subject to the law of Necessity, as they are that their Intelligence is. Can we conceive that Necessitarians would not be as solicitous to carry the question directly to the tribunal of Consciousness, as they now are to take it from that tribunal? When all men are as conscious that their Will is under the law of Liberty, as they are that their other faculties are under the relation of Necessity, no

wonder that Necessitarians anticipate the ruin of their cause, when the question is to be submitted to the bar of Consciousness. No wonder that they so solemnly protest against an appeal to that tribunal. Let the reader remember, however, that the moment the validity of the affirmations of Consciousness is denied, in respect to any question in mental science, it becomes infinite folly in us to reason at all on the subject; a folly just as great as it would be for a natural philosopher to reason about colors, after denying the validity of all affirmations of the eye, in respect to the phenomena about which he is to reason.

DOCTRINE OF LIBERTY ARGUED FROM THE EXISTENCE OF THE IDEA OF LIBERTY IN ALL MINDS.

III. I will present a third general argument in favor of the doctrine of Liberty; an argument, which, to my mind, is perfectly conclusive, but which differs somewhat from either of the forms of argumentation above presented. I argue the Liberty of the Will from the existence of the idea of Liberty in the human mind, in the form in which it is there found.

If the Will is not free, the idea of Liberty is wholly inapplicable to any phenomenon in existence whatever. Yet this idea is in the mind. The action of the Will in conformity to it is just as conceivable as its action in conformity to the idea of Necessity. It remains with the Necessitarian to account for the existence of this idea in the human mind, in consistency with his own theory. Here the following considerations present themselves demanding special attention.

1. The idea of Liberty, like that of Necessity, is a simple, and not a complex idea. This all will admit.

2. It could not have come into the mind from observation or reflection because all phenomena, external and internal, all the objects of observation and reflection, are, according to the doctrine of Necessity, not free, but necessary.

3. It could not have originated, as necessary ideas do, as the logical antecedents of the truths given by observation and reflection. For example, the idea of space, time, substance, and cause, are given in the Intelligence, as

the logical antecedents of the ideas of body, succession, phenomena, and events, all of which are truths derived from observation or reflection. Now the idea of Liberty, if the doctrine of Necessity is true, cannot have arisen in this way because all the objects of observation and reflection are, according to this doctrine, necessary, and therefore their logical antecedents must be. How shall we account, in consistency with this theory, for the existence of this idea in the mind? It came not from perception external, nor internal, nor as the logical antecedent or consequent of any truth thus perceived. Now if we admit the doctrine of Liberty as a truth of universal consciousness, we can give a philosophical account of the existence of the idea of Liberty in all minds. If we deny this doctrine, and consequently affirm that of Necessity, we may safely challenge any theologian or philosopher to give such an account of the existence of that idea in the mind. For all ideas, in the mind, do and must come from observation or reflection, or as the logical antecedents or consequents of ideas thus obtained. We have here an event without a cause, if the doctrine of Necessity is true.

4. All simple ideas, with the exception of that of Liberty, have realities within or around us, corresponding to them. If the doctrine of Necessity is true, we have one solitary idea of this character, that of Liberty, to which no reality corresponds. Whence this solitary intruder in the human mind?

The existence of this idea in the mind is proof demonstrative, that a reality corresponding to it does and must exist, and as this reality is found nowhere but in the Will, there it must be found. Almost all Necessitarians are, in philosophy, the disciples of Locke. With him, they maintain, that all ideas in the mind come from observation and reflection. Yet they maintain that there is in the mind one idea, that of Liberty, which never could thus have originated; because, according to their theory, no objects corresponding do or can exist, either as realities, or as the objects of observation or reflection. We have again an event without a cause, if the doctrine of Liberty is not true.

5. The relation of the ideas of Liberty and Necessity to those of obligation, merit and demerit, &c., next demand our attention. If the doctrine of Necessity is true, the idea of Liberty is, as we have seen, a chimera. With it the idea of obligation can have no connection or alliance; but must rest exclusively upon that of Necessity. Now, how happens it, that no man holding the doctrine of Liberty was ever known to deny that of obligation, or of merit

and demerit? How happens it, that the validity of neither of these ideas has ever, in any age or nation, been denied, except on the avowed authority of the doctrine of Necessity? Sceptics of the class who deny moral obligation, are universally avowed Necessitarians. We may safely challenge the world to produce a single exception to this statement. We may challenge the world to produce an individual in ancient or modern times who holds the doctrine of Liberty, and denies moral obligation, or an individual who denies moral obligation on any other ground than that of Necessity. Now, how can this fact be accounted for, that the ideas of obligation, merit and demerit, &c., universally attach themselves to a chimera, the idea of Liberty, and stand in such irreconcilable hostility to the only idea by which, as Necessitarians will have it, their validity is affirmed?

6. Finally, If the doctrine of Necessity is true, the phenomena of the Intelligence, Sensibility, and the Will, are given in Consciousness as alike necessary. The idea of Liberty, then, if it does exist in the mind, would not be likely to attach itself to either of these classes of phenomena; and if to either, it would be just as likely to attach itself to one class as to another. Now, how shall we account for the fact, that this idea always attaches itself to one of these classes of phenomena, those of the Will, and never to either of the others? How is it that all men agree in holding, that, in the circumstances of their occurrence, the phenomena of the Intelligence and Sensibility cannot but be what they are, while those of the Will may be otherwise than they are? Why, if this chimera, the idea of Liberty, attaches itself to either of these classes, does it not sometimes attach itself to the phenomena of the Intelligence or Sensibility, as well as to those of the Will? Here, once again, we have an event without a cause, a distinction without a difference, if the doctrine of Necessity is true. The facts before us can be accounted for only on the supposition, that the phenomena of the Intelligence and Sensibility are given in Consciousness as necessary, while those of the Will are given as free.

THE DOCTRINE OF LIBERTY, THE DOCTRINE OF THE BIBLE.

IV. We will now, in the fourth place, raise the inquiry, an inquiry very appropriate in its place, and having an important bearing upon our present investigations, whether the doctrine of the Will, above established, is the doctrine pre-supposed in the Bible? The following considerations will enable us to give a decisive answer to this inquiry.

1. If the doctrine of the Will here maintained is not, and consequently that of Necessity is, the doctrine pre-supposed in the Scriptures, then we have two revelations from God, the external and internal, in palpable contradiction to each other. As the works of God (see Rom. 1: 19, 20) are as real a revelation from him as the Bible, so are the necessary affirmations of our Intelligence. Now, in our inner being, in the depths of our Intelligence, the fact is perpetually revealed and affirmed--a fact which we cannot disbelieve, if we would--that we are not necessary but free agents. Suppose that, in the external revelation, the Scriptures, the fact is revealed and affirmed that we are not free but necessary agents. Has not God himself affirmed in one revelation what he has denied in another? Of what use can the internal revelation be, but to render us necessarily sceptical in respect to the external? Has the Most High given two such revelations as this?

2. In the Scriptures, man is presented as the subject, and, of course, as possessing those powers which render him the proper subject of command and prohibition, of obligation, of merit and demerit, and consequently of reward and punishment. Let us suppose that God has imparted to a being a certain constitution, and then placed him in a condition in which, in consequence of the necessary correlation between his constitution and circumstances, but one series of determinations are possible to him, and that series cannot but result. Can we conceive it proper in the Most High to prohibit that creature from pursuing the course which God himself has rendered it impossible for him not to pursue, and require him, under the heaviest sanctions, to pursue, under these identical circumstances, a different and opposite course--a course which the Creator has rendered it impossible for him to pursue? Is this the philosophy pre-supposed in the Bible? Does the Bible imply a system of mental philosophy which renders the terms, obligation, merit and demerit, void of all conceivable meaning, and which lays no other foundation for moral retributions but injustice and tyranny?

3. Let us now contemplate the doings of the Great Day revealed in the Scriptures, in the light of these two opposite theories. Let us suppose that, as the righteous and the wicked stand in distinct and separate masses before the Eternal One, the Most High says to the one class, "You, I myself placed in circumstances in which nothing but obedience was possible, and that you could not but render; and you, I placed in a condition in which nothing but

disobedience was possible to you, and that you could not but perpetrate. In consequence of these distinct and opposite courses, each of which I myself rendered unavoidable, you deserve and shall receive my eternal smiles; and you as richly deserve and shall therefore endure my eternal frowns." What would be the response of an assembled universe to a division based upon such a principle? Is this the principle on which the decisions of that Day are based? It must be so, if the doctrine of Liberty is not, and that of Necessity is, the doctrine of the Bible?

4. We will now contemplate another class of passages which have a bearing equally decisive upon our present inquiries. I refer to that class in which God expresses the deepest regret at the course which transgressors have pursued, and are still pursuing, and the most decisive unwillingness that they should pursue that course and perish. He takes a solemn oath, that he is not willing that they should take the course of disobedience and death, but that they should pursue a different and opposite course. God expresses no regret that they are in the circumstances in which they are, but that in those circumstances they should take the path of disobedience, and not that of obedience. Now, can we suppose, what must be true, if the doctrine of Necessity is the doctrine pre-supposed in the Bible, that God places his creatures in circumstances in which obedience is to them an impossibility, and in which they cannot but disobey, and then takes a solemn oath that he is not willing that they should disobey and perish, "but that they should turn from their evil way and live?" What is the meaning of the exclamation, "O that thou hadst hearkened to my commandment," if God himself had so conditioned the sinner as to render obedience an impossibility to him? Is this the philosophy of the Will pre-supposed in the Bible? On the other hand, how perfectly in place are all the passages under consideration, on the supposition that the doctrine of Liberty is the doctrine therein pre-supposed, and that consequently the obedience which God affirms Himself desirous that sinners should render, and his regret that they do not render, is always possible to them! One of the seven pillars of the Gospel is this very doctrine. Take it from the Bible, and we have "another Gospel."

5. One other class of passages claims special attention here. In the Scriptures, the Most High expresses the greatest astonishment that men should sin under the influences to which he has subjected them. He calls upon heaven and earth to unite with him in astonishment at the conduct of

men under those influences. "Hear, O heavens, and give ear, O earth," he exclaims, "for the Lord hath spoken; I have nourished and brought up children, and they have rebelled against me." Now, let us suppose, as the doctrine of Necessity affirms, that God has placed sinners under influences under which they cannot but sin. What must we think of his conduct in calling upon the universe to unite with him in astonishment, that under these influences they should sin--that is, take the only course possible to them, the course which they cannot but take? With the same propriety, he might place a mass of water on an inclined plane, and then call upon heaven and earth to unite with him in astonishment at the downward flow of the fluid. Is this the philosophy pre-supposed in the Bible?

SEC. 3. VIEWS OF NECESSITARIANS.

We are now prepared for a consideration of certain miscellaneous questions which have an important bearing upon our present inquiries.

NECESSITY AS HELD BY NECESSITARIANS.

I. The first inquiry that presents itself is this: Do Necessitarians hold the doctrine of Necessity as defined in this chapter? Do they really hold, in respect to every act of will, that, in the circumstances of its occurrence, that one act only is possible, and that cannot but arise? Is this, for example, the doctrine of Edwards? Is it the doctrine really held by those who professedly agree with him? I argue that it is:

1. Because they unanimously repudiate the doctrine of Liberty as here defined. They must, therefore, hold that of Necessity; inasmuch as no third relation is even conceivable or possible. If they deny that the phenomena of the Will fall under either of these relations, and still call themselves Necessitarians, they most hold to an inconceivable something, which themselves even do not understand and cannot define, and which has and can have no real existence.

2. Edwards has confounded the phenomena of the Will with those of the Sensibility which are necessary in the sense here defined. He must, therefore, hold that the characteristics of the latter class belong to those of the former.

3. Edwards represents the relation between motives and acts of Will, as being the same in kind as that which exists between causes and effects among external material substances. The former relation he designates by the words moral necessity; the latter, by that of natural, or philosophical, or physical necessity. Yet he says himself, that the difference expressed by these words "does not lie so much in the nature of the connection as in the two terms connected." The qualifying terms used, then, designate merely the nature of the antecedents and consequents, while the nature of the connection between them is, in all instances, the same, that of naked necessity.

4. Edwards himself represents moral necessity as just as absolute as physical, or natural necessity. "Moral necessity may be," he says, "as absolute as natural necessity. That is, the effect may be as perfectly connected with its moral cause as a natural necessary effect is with its natural cause."

5. Necessitarians represent the relation between motives and acts of Will as that of cause and effect; and for this reason necessary. "If," says Edwards, "every act of Will is excited by some motive, then that motive is the cause of that act of Will." "And if volitions are properly the effects of their motives, then they are necessarily connected with their motives." Now as the relation of cause and effect is necessary, in the sense of the term Necessity as above defined, Edwards must hold, and design to teach, that all acts of Will are necessary in this sense.

6. Necessitarians represent the connection between motives and acts of Will as being, in all instances, the same in kind as that which exists between volitions and external actions. "As external actions," says President Day, "are directed by the Will, so the Will itself is directed by influence." Now all admit, that the connection between volitions and external actions is necessary in this sense, that when we will such action it cannot but take place. No other act is, in the circumstances, possible. In the same sense, according to Necessitarians, is every act of Will necessarily connected with influence, or motives. We do Necessitarians no wrong, therefore, when we impute to them the doctrine of Necessity as here defined. In all cases of sin, they hold, that an individual is in circumstances in which none but sinful acts of Will are possible, and these he cannot but put forth; and that in these identical circumstances the sinner is under obligation infinite to put forth different and

opposite acts.

THE TERM, CERTAINTY, AS USED BY NECESSITARIANS.

II. We are prepared for another important inquiry, to wit: whether the words, certainty, moral certainty, &c., as used by Necessitarians, are identical in their meaning with that of Necessity as above defined? The doctrine of Necessity would never be received by the public at all, but for the language in which it is clothed, language which prevents the public seeing it as it is. At one time it is called Moral, in distinction from Natural Necessity. At another, it is said to be nothing but Certainty, or moral Certainty, &c. Now the question arises, what is this Certainty? Is it or is it not, real Necessity, and nothing else? That it is, I argue,

1. From the fact, as shown above, that there can possibly be no Certainty, which does not fall either under the relation of Liberty or Necessity as above defined. The Certainty of Necessitarians does not, according to their own showing, fall under the former relation: it must, therefore, fall under the latter. It must be naked Necessity, and nothing else.

2. While they have defined the term Necessity, and have not that of Certainty, they use the latter term as avowedly synonymous with the former. The latter, therefore, must be explained by the former, and not the former by the latter.

3. The Certainty which they hold is a certainty which avowedly excludes the possibility of different and opposite acts of Will under the influences, or motives, under which particular acts are put forth. The Certainty under consideration, therefore, is not necessity of a particular kind, a necessity consistent with liberty and moral obligation. It is the Necessity above defined, in all its naked deformity.

III. We are now prepared for a distinct statement of the doctrine of Ability, according to the Necessitarian scheme. Even the Necessitarians, with very few exceptions, admit, that in the absence of all power to do right or wrong, we can be under no obligation to do the one or avoid the other. "A man," says Pres. Day, "is not responsible for remaining in his place if he has no power to move. He is not culpable for omitting to walk, if he has no strength to walk. He is not under obligation to do anything for which he has not what Edwards calls natural power." It is very important for us to understand the nature of this ability, which lies at the foundation of moral obligation; to understand, I repeat, what this Ability is, according to the theory under consideration. This Ability, according to the doctrine of Liberty, has been well stated by Cousin, to wit: "The moment we take the resolution to do an action, we take it with a consciousness of being able to take a contrary resolution;" and by Dr. Dwight, who says of a man's sin, that it is "chosen by him unnecessarily, while possessed of a power to choose otherwise." The nature of this Ability, according to the Necessitarian scheme, has been stated with equal distinctness in the Christian Spectator. "If we take this term [Ability or Power] in the absolute sense, as including all the antecedents to a given volition, there is plainly no such thing as power to the contrary; for in this sense of the term," as President Day states, "a man never has power to do anything but what he actually performs." "In this comprehensive, though rather unusual sense of the word," says President Day, "a man has not power to do anything which he does not do." The meaning of the above extracts cannot be mistaken. Nor can any one deny that they contain a true exposition of the doctrine of Necessity, to wit: that under the influences under which men do will, and consequently act, it is absolutely impossible for them to will and act differently from what they do. In what sense, then, have they power to will and act differently according to this doctrine? To this question President Day has given a correct and definite answer. "The man who wills in a particular way, under the influence of particular feelings, might will differently under a different influence."

Now, what is the doctrine of Ability, according to this scheme? A man, for example, commits an act of sin. He ought, in the stead of that act, to have put forth an act of obedience. Without the power to render this obedience, as President Day admits, there can be no obligation to do it. When the Necessitarian says, that the creature, when he sins, has power to obey, he means, not that under the influence under which the act of sin is committed, the creature has power to obey; but that under a different influence he might obey. But mark, it is under the identical influence under which a man does sin, and under which, according to the doctrine of Necessity, he cannot but sin, that he is required not to sin. Now how can a man's ability, and obligation not to sin under a given influence, grow out of the fact, that, under a different influence, an influence under which he cannot but do right, he might not sin?

This is all the ability and ground of obligation as far as Ability, Natural Ability as it is called, is concerned, which the doctrine of Necessity admits. A man is, by a power absolutely irresistible, placed in circumstances in which he cannot possibly but sin. In these circumstances, it is said, that he has natural ability not to sin, and consequently ought not to do it. Why? Because, to his acting differently, no change in his nature or powers is required. These are "perfect and entire, wanting nothing." All that is required is, that his circumstances be changed, and then he might not sin. "In what sense," asks President Day, "is it true, that a man has power to will the contrary of what he actually wills? He has such power that, with a sufficient inducement, he will make an opposite choice." Is not this the strangest idea of Natural Ability as constituting the foundation of obligation, of which the human mind ever tried to conceive? In illustration, let us suppose that a man, placed in the city of New York, cannot but sin; placed in that of Boston, he cannot but be holy, and that the fact whether he is in the one or the other city depends upon the irresistible providence of God. He is placed in New York where he cannot but sin. He is told that he ought not to do it, and that he is highly guilty for not being perfectly holy. It is also asserted that he has all the powers of moral agency, all the ability requisite to lay the foundation for the highest conceivable obligation to be holy. What is the evidence? he asks. Is it possible for me, in my present circumstances, to avoid sin? and in my present circumstances, you know, I cannot but be. I acknowledge, the Necessitarian says, that under present influences, you cannot but sin, and that you cannot but be subject to these influences. Still, I affirm, that you have all the powers of moral agency, all the natural ability requisite to obedience, and to the highest conceivable obligation to obedience. Because, in the first place, even in New York, you could obey if you chose. You have, therefore, natural, though not moral, power to obey. But stop, friend, right here. When you say that I might obey, if I chose, I would ask, if choosing, as in the command, "choose life," is not the very thing required of me? When, therefore, you affirm that I might obey, if I chose, does it not mean, in reality, that I might choose, if I should choose? Is not your Natural Ability this, that I might obey if I did obey?[2] I cannot deny, the Necessitarian replies, that you have correctly stated this doctrine. Permit me to proceed in argument, however. In the next place, all that you need in order to be holy as required, is a change, not of your powers, but of the influences which control the action of those powers. With no change in your constitution or powers, you need only to be placed in Boston instead of New York, and there you cannot but be holy. Is it not as clear as light, therefore, that you have now all the powers of moral agency, all the ability requisite to the highest conceivable obligation to be holy instead of sinful?

I fully understand you, the sinner replies. But remember, that it is not in Boston, where, as you acknowledge, I cannot be, that I am required not to sin; but here, in New York, where I cannot but be, and cannot possibly but sin. It is here, and not somewhere else, that I am required not to sin. How can the fact, that if I were in Boston, where I could not but be holy, I might not sin, prove, that here, in New York, I have any ability, either natural or moral--am under any obligation whatever--not to sin? These are the difficulties which press upon me. How do you remove them according to your theory?

I can give no other answer, the Necessitarian replies, than that already given. If that does not silence for ever every excuse for sin in your mind, it is wholly owing to the perverseness of your heart, to its bitter hostility to the truth. I may safely appeal to the Necessitarian himself, whether I have not here given an uncaricatured expose of his theory.

SINFUL INCLINATIONS.

IV. When pressed with such appalling difficulties as these, the Necessitarian falls back, in self-justification, upon the reason why the sinner cannot be holy. The only reason, it is said, why the sinner does not do as he ought is, not the want of power, but the strength of his sinful inclinations. Shall he plead these in excuse for sin? By no means. They constitute the very essence of the sinner's guilt. Let it be borne in mind, that, according to the doctrine of Necessity, such is the connection between the nature, or constitution of the sinner's mind--a nature which God has given him, and the influences under which he is placed by Divine Providence--that none but these very inclinations are possible to him, and these cannot but exist. From these inclinations, sinful acts of Will cannot but arise. How is the matter helped, as far as ability and obligation, on the part of the sinner, are concerned, by throwing the guilt back from acts of Will upon inclinations equally necessary?

NECESSARIAN DOCTRINE OF LIBERTY.

The real liberty of the Will, according to the Necessitarian scheme, next demands our attention. All admit that Liberty is an essential condition of moral obligation. In what sense, then, is or is not, man free, according to the doctrine of Necessity?

"The plain and obvious meaning of the words Freedom and Liberty," says President Edwards, "is power, opportunity, or advantage, that any one has to do as he pleases. Or, in other words, his being free from hinderance or impediment in the way of doing or conducting in any respect as he wills. And the contrary to Liberty, whatever name we please to call that by, is a person's being hindered, or unable to conduct as he will, or being necessitated to do otherwise." "The only idea, indeed, that we can form of free-agency, or of freedom of Will," says Abercrombie, "is, that it consists in a man's being able to do what he wills, or to abstain from doing what he will not. Necessary agency, on the other hand, would consist in a man's being compelled, by a force from without, to do what he will not, or prevented from doing what he wills."

With these definitions all Necessitarians agree. This is all the Liberty known, or conceivable, according to their theory. Liberty does not consist in the power to choose in one or the other of two or more different and opposite directions, under the same influence. It is found wholly and exclusively in the connection between the act of Will, considered as the antecedent, and the effort, external or internal, considered as the consequent. On this definition I remark,

1. That it presents the idea of Liberty as distinguished from Servitude, rather than Liberty as distinguished from Necessity. A man is free, in the first sense of the term, when no external restraints hinder the carrying out of the choice within. This, however, has nothing to do with Liberty, as distinguished from Necessity.

2. If this is the only sense in which a man is free, then, in the language of a very distinguished philosopher, "if you cut off a man's little finger, you thereby annihilate so much of his free agency;" because, in that case, you abridge so much his power to do as he chooses. Is this Liberty, the only liberty of man, a liberty which may be destroyed by chains, bolts, and bars? Is this Liberty as distinguished from Necessity the liberty which lays the foundation of moral obligation?

3. If this is the only sense in which man is free, then dire Necessity reigns throughout the entire domain of human agency. If all acts of Will are the necessary consequents of the influences to which the mind is at the time subjected, much more must a like necessity exist between all acts of Will and their consequents, external and internal. This has been already shown. The mind, then, with all its acts and states, exists in a chain of antecedents and consequents, causes and effects, linked together in every part and department by a dire necessity. This is all the Liberty that this doctrine knows or allows us; a Liberty to choose as influences necessitate us to choose, and to have such acts of Will followed by certain necessary consequents, external and internal. In this scheme, the idea of Liberty, which all admit must have a location somewhere, or obligation, is a chimera; this idea, I say, after "wandering through dry places, seeking rest and finding none," at length is driven to a location where it finds its grave, and not a living habitation.

4. It is to me a very strange thing, that Liberty, as the foundation of moral obligation, should be located here. Because that acts of Will are followed by certain corresponding necessary consequents external and internal, therefore we are bound to put forth given acts of Will, whatever the influences acting upon us may be, and however impossible it may be to put forth those acts under those influences! Did ever a greater absurdity dance in the brain of a philosopher or theologian?

5. The public are entirely deceived by this definition, and because they are deceived as to the theory intended by it, do they admit it as true? Suppose any man in the common walks of life were asked what he means, when he says, he can do as he pleases, act as he chooses, &c. Does this express your meaning? When you will to walk, rather than sit, for example, no other volition is at the time possible, and this you must put forth, and that when you have put forth this volition, you cannot but walk. Is this your idea, when you say, you can do as you please? No, he would say. That is not my idea at all. If that is true, man is not a free agent at all. What men in general really mean when they say, they can do as they please, and are therefore free, is, that when they put forth a given act of Will, and for this reason conduct in a given manner, they may in the same circumstances put forth different and opposite determinations, and consequently act in a different and opposite manner from what they do.

VI. The argument of Necessitarians in respect to the practical tendencies of their doctrine demands a passing notice. All acts of the Will, they say, are indeed necessary under the circumstances in which they occur; but then we should learn the practical lesson not to place ourselves in the circumstances where we shall be liable to act wrong. To this I reply:

1. That on the hypothesis before us, our being in the circumstances which originate a given choice, is as necessary as the choice itself. For I am in those circumstances either by an overruling Providence over which I have no control, or by previous acts of the Will rendered necessary by such Providence. Hence the difficulty remains in all its force.

2. The solution assumes the very principle denied, that is, that our being in circumstances which originate particular acts of choice is not necessary. Else why tell an individual he is to blame for being in such circumstances, and not to place himself there again?

GROUND WHICH NECESSITARIANS ARE BOUND TO TAKE IN RESPECT TO THE DOCTRINE OF ABILITY.

VII. We are now fully prepared to state the ground which Necessitarians of every school are bound to take in respect to the doctrine of Ability. It is to deny that doctrine wholly, to take the open and broad ground, that, according to any appropriate signification of the words, it is absolutely impossible for men to will, and consequently to act, differently from what they do; that when they do wrong, they always do it, with the absolute impossibility of doing right; and that when they do right, there is always an equal impossibility of their doing wrong. If men have not power to will differently from what they do, it is undeniably evident that they have no power whatever to act differently: because there is an absolutely necessary connection between volitions and their consequents, external actions. The doctrine of Necessity takes away wholly all ability from the creature to will differently from what he does. It therefore totally annihilates his ability to act differently. What, then, according to the theory of Necessity, becomes of the doctrine of Ability? It is annihilated. It is impossible for us to find for it a "local habitation or a name." As honest men, Necessitarians are bound to proclaim the fact. They are bound to proclaim the doctrine, that, in requiring men to be holy, under influences under which they do sin, and cannot but sin (as it is true of all sinful acts according to their theory), God requires of them absolute impossibilities, and then dooms them to perdition for not performing such impossibilities.

The subterfuge to which Necessitarians resort here, will not avail them at all, to wit: that men are to blame for not doing right, because, they might do it if they chose. To will right is the thing, and the only thing really required of them. The above maxim therefore amounts, as we have already seen, to this: Men are bound to do, that is, to will, what is right, because if they should will what is right, they would will what is right.

DOCTRINE OF NECESSITY, AS REGARDED BY NECESSITARIANS OF DIFFERENT SCHOOLS.

VIII. Two schools divide the advocates of Necessity. According to one class, God produces in men all their volitions and acts, both sinful and holy, by the direct exertion of his own omnipotence. Without the Divine agency, men, they hold, are wholly incapable of all volitions and actions of every kind. With it, none but those which God produces can arise, and these cannot but arise. This is the scheme of Divine efficiency, as advocated by Dr. Emmons and others.

According to the other school, God does not, in all instances, produce volitions and actions by his own direct agency, but by creating in creatures a certain nature or constitution, and then subjecting them to influences from which none but particular volitions and acts which they do put forth can result, and these must result. According to a large portion of this school, God, either by his own direct agency, or by sustaining their laws of natural generation, produces in men the peculiar nature which they do possess, and then imputes to them infinite guilt, not only for this nature, but for its necessary results, sinful feelings, volitions, and actions.

Such are these two schemes. In the two following particulars, they perfectly harmonize. 1. All acts of Will, together with their effects, external and internal, in the circumstances of their occurrence, cannot but be what they are. 2. The ground of this necessity is the agency of God, in the one instance producing these effects directly and immediately, and in the other producing the same results, mediately, by giving existence to a constitution and influences from which such results cannot but arise. They differ only in respect to the immediate ground of this necessity, the power of God, according to the former, producing the effects directly, and according to the latter, indirectly. According to both, all our actions sustain the same essential relation to the Divine Will, that of Necessity.

Now while these two theories so perfectly harmonize, in all essential particulars, strange to tell, the advocates of one regard the other as involving the most monstrous absurdities conceivable. For God to produce, through the energies of his own omnipotence, human volitions, and then to impute infinite guilt to men for what he himself has produced in them, what a horrid sentiment that is, exclaims the advocate of constitutional depravity. For God to create in men a sinful nature, and then impute to them infinite guilt for what he has himself created, together with its unavoidable results, what horrid tyranny such a sentiment imputes to the Most High, exclaims the advocate of Divine efficiency, in his turn.

The impartial, uncommitted spectator, on the other hand, perceives most distinctly the same identical absurdities in both these theories. He knows perfectly, that it can make no essential difference, whether God produces a result directly, or by giving existence to a constitution and influences from which it cannot but arise. If one theory involves injustice and tyranny, the other must involve the same. Let me here add, that the reprobation with which each of the classes above named regards the sentiments of the other, is a sentence of reprobation passed (unconsciously to be sure) upon the doctrine of Necessity itself which is common to both. For if this one element is taken out of either theory, there is nothing left to render it abhorrent to any mind. It is thus that Necessitarians themselves, without exception, pass sentence of condemnation upon their own theory, by condemning it, in every system in which they meet with it except their own. There is not a man on earth, that has not in some form or other passed sentence of reprobation upon this system. Let any man, whatever, contemplate any theory but the one he has himself adopted, any theory that involves this element, and he will instantly fasten upon this one feature as the characteristic which vitiates the whole theory, and renders it deserving of universal reprobation. It is thus that unsophisticated Nature expresses her universal horror at a system which

"Binding nature fast in fate, Enslaves the human Will."

Unsophisticated Nature abhors this doctrine infinitely more than she was ever conceived to abhor a vacuum. Can a theory which the universal Intelligence thus agrees in reprobating, as involving the most horrid absurdity and tyranny conceivable, be the only true one?

CHAPTER IV.

EXTENT AND LIMITS OF THE LIBERTY OF THE WILL.

WHILE it is maintained, that, in the sense defined in the preceding chapter, the Will is free, it is also affirmed that, in other respects, it is not free at all. It should be borne distinctly in mind, that, in the respects in which the Will is subject to the law of Liberty, its liberty is absolute. It is in no sense subject to the law of Necessity. So far, also, as it is subject to the law of Necessity, it is in no sense free. What then are the extent and limits of the Liberty of the Will?

1. In the absence of Motives, the Will cannot act at all. To suppose the opposite would involve a contradiction. It would suppose the action of the Will in the direction of some object, in the absence of all objects towards which such action can be directed.

2. The Will is not free in regard to what the Motives presented shall be, in view of which its determinations shall be formed. Motives exist wholly independent of the Will. Nor does it depend at all upon the Will, what Motives shall be presented for its election. It is free only in respect to the particular determinations it shall put forth, in reference to the Motives actually presented.

3. Whenever a Motive, or object of choice, is presented to the mind, the Will is necessitated, by the presentation of the object, to act in some direction. It must yield or refuse to yield to the Motive. But such refusal is itself a positive act. So far, therefore, the Will is wholly subject to the law of Necessity. It is free, not in respect to whether it shall, or shall not, choose at all when a Motive is presented; but in respect to what it shall choose. I, for example, offer a merchant a certain sum, for a piece of goods. Now while it is equally possible for him to receive or reject the offer, one or the other determination he must form. In the first respect, he is wholly free. In the latter, he is not free

in any sense whatever. The same holds true in respect to all objects of choice presented to the mind. Motive necessitates the Will to act in some direction; while, in all deliberate Moral Acts at least, it leaves either of two or more different and opposite determinations equally possible to the mind.

4. Certain particular volitions may be rendered necessary by other, and what may be termed general, determinations. For example, a determination to pursue a particular course of conduct, may render necessary all particular volitions requisite to carry this general purpose into accomplishment. It renders them necessary in this sense, that if the former does exist, the latter must exist. A man, for example, determines to pass from Boston to New York with all possible expedition. This determination remaining unchanged, all the particular volitions requisite to its accomplishment cannot but exist. The general and controlling determination, however, may, at any moment, be suspended. To perpetuate or suspend it, is always in the power of the Will.

5. I will here state a conjecture, viz.: that there are in the primitive developments of mind, as well as in all primary acts of attention, certain necessary spontaneities of the Will, as well as of other powers of the mind. Is it not in consequence of such actions, that the mind becomes first conscious of the power of volition, and is it not now necessary for us under certain circumstances to give a certain degree of attention to phenomena which appear within and around us? My own convictions are, that such circumstances often do occur. Nor is such a supposition inconsistent with the great principle maintained in this Treatise. This principle is, that Liberty and Accountability, in other words, Free, and Moral Agency, are co-extensive.

6. Nor does Liberty, as here defined, imply, that the mind, antecedently to all acts of Will, shall be in a state of indifference, unimpelled by feeling, or the affirmations of the Intelligence, more strongly in one direction than another. The Will exists in a tri-unity with the Intelligence and Sensibility. Its determinations may be in harmony with the Sensibility, in opposition to Intelligence, or with the Intelligence in opposition to the Sensibility. But while it follows either in distinction from the other, under the same identical influences, different and opposite determinations are equally possible. However the Will may be influenced, whether its determinations are in the direction of the strongest impulse, or opposed to it, it never, in deliberate moral determination, puts forth particular acts, because, that in these

circumstances, no others are possible. In instances comparatively few, can we suppose that the mind, antecedently to acts of Will, is in a state of indifference, unimpelled in one direction in distinction from others, or equally impelled in the direction of different and opposite determinations. Indifference is in no such sense an essential or material condition of Liberty. How ever strongly the Will may be impelled in the direction of particular determinations, it is still in the possession of the highest conceivable freedom, if it is not thereby necessitated to act in one direction in distinction from all others.

7. I now refer to one other fixed law under the influence of which the Will is always necessitated to act. It is the law of habit. Action in any one direction always generates a tendency to subsequent action in the same direction under similar influences. This tendency may be increased, till it becomes so strong as to render action in the same direction in all future time really, although contingently, certain. The certainty thus granted will always be of such a nature as consists fully with the relation of Liberty. It can never, while moral agency continues, come under the relation of Necessity. Still the certainty is real. Thus the mind, by a continued course of well or ill doing, may generate such fixed habits, as to render subsequent action in the same direction perfectly certain, during the entire progress of its future being. Every man, while conscious of freedom, should be fully aware of the existence of this law, and it should surely lead him to walk thoughtfully along the borders of "the undiscovered country," his location in which he is determining by the habits of thought, feeling, and action, he is now generating.

STRONGEST MOTIVE--REASONING IN A CIRCLE.

A singular instance of reasoning in a circle on the part of Necessitarians, in respect to what they call the strongest Motive, demands a passing notice here. One of their main arguments in support of their doctrine is based upon the assumption, that the action of the Will is always in the direction of the strongest Motive. When, however, we ask them, which is the strongest Motive, their reply in reality is, that it is the Motive in the direction of which the Will does act. "The strength of a Motive," says President Day, "is not its prevailing, but the power by which it prevails. Yet we may very properly measure this power by the actual result." Again, "We may measure the comparative strength of Motives of different kinds, from the results to which they lead; just as we learn the power of different causes, from the effects which they produce:" that is, we are not to determine, a priori, nor by an appeal to consciousness, which of two or more Motives presented is the strongest. We are to wait till the Will does act, and then assume that the Motive, in the direction of which it acts, is the strongest. From the action of the Will in the direction of that particular Motive, we are finally to infer the truth of the doctrine of Necessity. The strongest Motive, according to the above definition, is the motive to which the Will does yield. The argument based upon the truism, that the Will always acts in the direction of this Motive, that is, the Motive towards which it does act, the argument, I say, put into a logical form, would stand thus. If the action of the Will is always in the direction of the strongest Motive, that is, if it always follows the Motive it does follow, it is governed by the law of Necessity. Its action is always in the direction of this Motive, that is, it always follows the Motive it does follow. The Will is therefore governed by the law of Necessity. How many philosophers and theologians have become "rooted and grounded" in the belief of this doctrine, under the influence of this sophism, a sophism which, in the first instance, assumes the doctrine as true, and then moves round in a vicious circle to demonstrate its truth.

CHAPTER V.

THE GREATEST APPARENT GOOD.

SECTION I.

WE now come to a consideration of one of the great questions bearing upon our personal investigations--the proposition maintained by Necessitarians, as a chief pillar of their theory, that "the Will always is as the greatest apparent good."

PHRASE DEFINED.

The first inquiry which naturally arises here is What is the proper meaning of this proposition?

In reply, I answer, that it must mean one of these three things.

1. That the Will is always, in all its determinations, conformed to the dictates of the Intelligence, choosing those things only which the Intelligence affirms to be best. Or,

2. That the determinations of the Will are always in conformity to the impulse of the Sensibility, that is, that its action is always in the direction of the strongest feeling. Or,

3. In conformity to the dictates of the Intelligence, and the impulse of the Sensibility combined, that is that the Will never acts at all, except when impelled by the Intelligence and Sensibility both in the same direction.

MEANING OF THIS PHRASE ACCORDING TO EDWARDS.

The following passage leaves no room for doubt in respect to the meaning which Edwards attaches to the phrase, "the greatest apparent good." "I have chosen," he says, "rather to express myself thus, that the Will always is as the greatest apparent good, or as what appears most agreeable, than to say, that the Will is determined by the greatest apparent good, or by what seems most agreeable; because an appearing most agreeable or pleasing to the mind, and the mind's preferring and choosing, seem hardly to be properly and perfectly distinct." Here undeniably, the words, choosing, preferring, "appearing most agreeable or pleasing," and "the greatest apparent good," are defined as identical in their meaning. Hence in another place, he adds, "If strict propriety of speech be insisted on, it may more properly be said, that the voluntary action which is the immediate consequence and fruit of the mind's volition and choice, is determined by that which appears most agreeable, than by the preference or choice itself." The reason is obvious. Appearing most agreeable or pleasing, and preference or choice, had been defined as synonymous in their meaning. To say, therefore, that preference or choice is determined by "what appears most agreeable or pleasing," would be equivalent to the affirmation, that choice determines choice. "The act of volition itself," he adds, "is always determined by that in or about the mind's view of an object, which causes it to appear most agreeable," or what is by definition the same thing, causes it to be chosen. The phrases, "the greatest apparent good," and "appearing most agreeable or pleasing to the mind," and the words, choosing, preferring, &c., are therefore, according to Edwards, identical in their meaning. The proposition, "the Will is always as the greatest apparent good," really means nothing more nor less than this, that Will always chooses as it chooses. The famous argument based upon this proposition in favor of the doctrine of Necessity may be thus expressed. If the Will always is as the greatest apparent good, that is, if the Will always chooses as it chooses, it is governed by the law of Necessity. The Will is as the greatest apparent good, that is, it always chooses as it chooses. Therefore it is governed by this law. By this very syllogism, multitudes have supposed that the doctrine of Necessity has been established with all the distinctness and force of demonstration.

The question now returns, Is "the Will always as the greatest apparent good," in either of the senses of the phrase as above defined?

THE WILL NOT ALWAYS AS THE DICTATES OF THE INTELLIGENCE.

I. Is the Will then as the greatest apparent good in this sense, that all its determinations are in conformity to the dictates of the Intelligence. Does the Will never harmonize with the Sensibility in opposition to the Intelligence? Has no intelligent being, whether sinful or holy, ever done that which his Intellect affirmed at the time, that he ought not to do, and that it was best for him not to do? I answer,

1. Every man who has ever violated moral obligation knows, that he has followed the impulse of desire, in opposition to the dictates of his Intelligence. What individual that has ever perpetrated such deeds has not said, and cannot say with truth, "I know the good, and approve it; yet follow the bad?" Take a matter of fact. A Spanish nobleman during the early progress of the Reformation, became fully convinced, that the faith of the Reformers was true, and his own false, and that his salvation depended upon his embracing the one and rejecting the other. Yet martyrdom would be the result of such a change. While balancing this question, in the depths of his own mind, he trembled with the greatest agitation. His sovereign who was present, asked the cause. The reply was, "the martyr's crown is before me, and I have not Christian fortitude enough to take it." He died a few weeks subsequent, without confessing the truth. Did he obey his Intelligence, or Sensibility there? Was not the conflict between the two, and did not the latter prevail? In John 12: 42, 43, we have a fact revealed, in which men were convinced of the truth,

and yet, because "they loved the praise of men more than the praise of God," they did not confess, but denied the truth, a case therefore in which they followed the impulse of desire, in opposition to the dictates of the Intelligence. The Will then is not "always as the greatest apparent good," in this sense, that its action is always in the direction of the dictates of the Intelligence.

2. If this is so, sin, in all instances, is a mere blunder, a necessary result of a necessary misjudgment of the Intelligence? Is it so? Can the Intelligence affirm that a state of moral impurity is better than a state of moral rectitude? How easy it would be, in every instance, to "convert a sinner from the error of his way," if all that is requisite is to carry his Intellect in favor of truth and righteousness? Who does not know, that the great difficulty lies in the enslavement of the Will to a depraved Sensibility?

3. If the Will of all Intelligents is always in harmony with the Intellect, then I affirm that there is not, and never has been, any such thing as sin, or ill desert, in the universe. What more can be said of God, or of any being ever so pure, than that he has always done what his Intellect affirmed to be best? What if the devil, and all creatures called sinners, had always done the same thing? Where is the conceivable ground for the imputation of moral guilt to them?

4. If all acts of Will are always in perfect harmony with the Intelligence, and in this sense, "as the greatest apparent good," then, when the Intellect affirms absolutely that there can be no ground of preference between two objects, there can be no choice between them. But we are, in fact, putting forth every day just such acts of Will, selecting one object in distinction from another, when the Intellect affirms their perfect equality, or affirms absolutely, that there is and can be no perceived ground of preference between them. I receive a letter, I will suppose, from a friend, informing me that he has just taken from a bank two notes, perfectly new and of the same value, that one now lies in the east and the other in the west corner of his drawer, that I may have one and only one of them, the one that I shall name by return of mail, and that I must designate one or the other, or have neither. Here are present to my Intelligence two objects absolutely equal. Their location is a matter of indifference, equally absolute. Now if as the proposition "the Will is always as the greatest apparent good," affirms, I cannot select one object in distinction from another, without a perceived

ground for such selection, I could not possibly, in the case supposed, say which bill I would have. Yet I make the selection without the least conceivable embarrassment. I might mention numberless cases, of daily occurrence, of a nature precisely similar. Every child that ever played at "odd or even," knows perfectly the possibility of selecting between objects which are, to the Intelligence, absolutely equal.

I will now select a case about which there can possibly be no mistake. Space we know perfectly to be absolutely infinite. Space in itself is in all parts alike. So must it appear to the mind of God. Now when God determined to create the universe, he must have resolved to locate its centre in some one point of space in distinction from all others. At that moment, there was present to the Divine Intelligence an infinite number of points, all and each absolutely equally eligible. Neither point could have been selected, because it was better than any other: for all were equal. So they must have appeared to God. Now if the "Will is always as the greatest apparent good," in the sense under consideration, God could not in this case make the selection, and consequently could not create the universe. He did make the selection, and did create. The Will, therefore, is not, in this sense, "always as the greatest apparent good."

THE WILL NOT ALWAYS AS THE STRONGEST DESIRE.

II. Is the "Will always as the greatest apparent good" in this sense, that it is always as the strongest desire, or as the strongest impulse of the Sensibility? Does the Will never harmonize with the Intelligence, in opposition to the Sensibility, as well as with the Sensibility in opposition to the Intelligence? If this is not so, then--

1. It would be difficult to define self-denial according to the ordinary acceptation of the term. What is self-denial but placing the Will with the Intelligence, in opposition to the Sensibility? How often in moral reformations do we find almost nothing else but this, an inflexible purpose placed directly before an almost crushing and overwhelming tide of feeling and desire?

2. When the Will is impelled in different directions, by conflicting feelings, it could not for a moment be in a state of indecision, unless we suppose these conflicting feelings to be absolutely equal in strength up to the moment of

decision. Who believes that? Who believes that his feelings are in all instances in a state of perfect equilibrium up to the moment of fixed determination between two distinct and opposite courses? This must be the case, if the action of the Will is always as the strongest feeling, and in this sense as the "greatest apparent good." How can Necessitarians meet this argument? Will they pretend that, in all instances, up to the moment of decisive action, the feelings impelling the Will in different directions are always absolutely equal in strength? This must be, if the Will is always as the strongest feeling.

3. When the feelings are in a state of perfect equilibrium, there can possibly, on this supposition, be no choice at all. The feelings often are, and must be, in this state, even when we are necessitated to act in some direction. The case of the bank notes above referred to, presents an example of this kind. As the objects are in the mind's eye absolutely equal, to suppose that the feelings should, in such a case, impel the Will more strongly in the direction of the one than the other, is to suppose an event without a cause, inasmuch as the Sensibility is governed by the law of Necessity. If A and B are to the Intelligence, in all respects, absolutely equal, how can the Sensibility impel the Will towards A instead of B? What is an event without a cause, if this is not? Contemplate the case in respect to the location of the universe above supposed. Each point of space was equally present to God, and was in itself, and was perceived and affirmed to be, equally eligible with all the others. How could a stronger feeling arise in the direction of one point in distinction from others, unless we suppose that God's Sensibility is not subject to the law of Necessity, a position which none will assume, or that here was an event without a cause? When, therefore, God did select this one point in distinction from all the others, that determination could not have been either in the direction of what the Intelligence affirmed to be best, nor of the strongest feeling. The proposition, therefore, that "the Will always is as the greatest apparent good," is in both the senses above defined demonstrably false.

4. Of the truth of this every one is aware when he appeals to his own Consciousness. In the amputation of a limb, for example, who does not know that if an individual, at the moment when the operation commences, should yield to the strongest feeling, he would refuse to endure it? He can pass through the scene, only by placing an inflexible purpose directly across the current of feeling. How often do we hear individuals affirm, "If I should follow

my feelings, I should do this; if I should follow my judgment, I should do that." In all such instances, we have the direct testimony of consciousness, that the action of the Will is not always in the direction of the strongest feeling: because its action is sometimes consciously in the direction of the Intelligence, in opposition to such feelings; and at others, in the conscious presence of such feelings, the Will remains, for periods longer or shorter, undecided in respect to the particular course which shall be pursued.

THE WILL NOT ALWAYS AS THE INTELLIGENCE AND SENSIBILITY COMBINED.

III. Is not the Will always as the greatest apparent good in this sense, that its determinations are always as the affirmations of the Intelligence and the impulse of the Sensibility combined? That it is not, I argue for two reasons.

1. If this was the case, when the Intelligence and Sensibility are opposed to each other--a fact of very frequent occurrence,--there could be no acts of Will in either direction. The Will must remain in a state of absolute inaction, till these belligerent powers settle their differences, and unite in impelling the Will in some particular direction. But we know that the Will can, and often does, act in the direction of the Intelligence or Sensibility, when the affirmations of one and the impulses of the other are in direct opposition to each other.

2. When both the Intellect and Sensibility, as in the cases above cited, are alike indifferent, there can be, on the present hypothesis, no acts of Will whatever. Under these identical circumstances, however, the Will does act. The hypothesis, therefore, falls to the ground.

I conclude, then, that the proposition, "the Will is always as the greatest apparent good," is either a mere truism, having no bearing at all upon our present inquiries, or that it is false.

In the discussion of the above propositions, the doctrine of Liberty has received a full and distinct illustration. The action of the Will is sometimes in the direction of the Intelligence, in opposition to the Sensibility, and sometimes in the direction of the Sensibility, in opposition to the Intelligence, and never in the direction of either, because it must be. Sometimes it acts where the Sensibility and Intelligence both harmonize, or are alike indifferent.

When also the Will acts in the direction of the Intelligence or Sensibility, it is not necessitated to follow, in all instances, the highest affirmation, nor the strongest desire.

SEC. II--MISCLLANEOUS TOPICS.

NECESSITARIAN ARGUMENT.

I. We are now prepared to appreciate the Necessitarian argument, based upon the assumption, that "the Will always is as the greatest apparent good." This assumption is the great pillar on which that doctrine rests. Yet the whole argument based upon it is a perpetual reasoning in a circle. Ask the Necessitarian to give the grand argument in favor of his doctrine. His answer is, because "the Will always is as the greatest apparent good." Cite now such facts as those stated above in contradiction of his assumption, and his answer is ready. There must be, in all such cases, some perceived or felt ground of preference, or there could be no act of Will in the case. There must have been, for example, some point in space more eligible than any other for the location of the universe, and this must have been the reason why God selected the one he did. Ask him why he makes this declaration? His reply is, because "the Will is always as the greatest apparent good." Thus this assumption becomes premise or conclusion, just as the exigence of the theory based upon it demands. Nothing is so convenient and serviceable as such an assumption, when one has a very difficult and false position to sustain. But who does not see, that it is a most vicious reasoning in a circle? To assume the proposition, "the Will always is as the greatest apparent good," in the first instance, as the basis of a universal theory, and then to assume the truth of that proposition as the basis of the explanation of particular facts, which contradict that theory, what is reasoning in a circle if this is not? No one has a right to assume this proposition as true at all, until he has first shown that it is affirmed by all the phenomena of the Will. On its authority he has no right to explain a solitary phenomenon. To do it is not only to reason in a circle, but to beg the question at issue.

MOTIVES CAUSE ACTS OF WILL, IN WHAT SENSE.

II. We are also prepared to notice another assumption of President Edwards, which, if admitted in the sense in which he assumes it as true, necessitates the admission of the Necessitarian scheme, to wit: that the determination of the Will is always caused by the Motive present to the mind for putting forth that determination. "It is that motive," he says, "which, as it stands in the view of the mind, is the strongest which determines the Will." Again, "that every act of the Will has some cause, and consequently (by what has been already proved) has a necessary connection with its cause, and so is necessary by a necessity of connection and consequence, is evident by this, that every act of Will, whatsoever, is excited by some motive." "But if every act of the Will is excited by some motive, then that motive is the cause of that act of the Will." "And if volitions are properly the effects of their motives, then they are necessarily connected with their motives."

If we grant the principle here assumed, the conclusion follows of necessity. But let us inquire in what sense motive and volition sustain to each other the relation of cause and effect. The presence and action of one power causes the action of another, so far, and so far only, as it necessitates such action; and causes its action in a particular direction, so far only as it necessitates its action in that direction, in opposition to every other. Now the action of one power may cause the action of another, in one or both these ways.

1. It may necessitate its action, and necessitate it in one direction in opposition to any and every other. In this sense, fire causes the sensation of pain. It necessitates the action of the Sensibility, and in that one direction. Or,

2. One power may necessitate the action of another power, but not necessitate its action in one direction in opposition to any or all others. We have seen, in a former chapter, that the Motive causes the action of the Will in this sense only, that it necessitates the Will to act in some direction, but not in one direction in distinction from another. Now the error of President Edwards lies in confounding these two senses of the word cause. He assumes that when one power causes the action of another in any sense, it must in every sense. It is readily admitted, that in one sense the Motive causes the action of the Will. But when we ask for the reason or cause of any one particular choice in distinction from another, we find it, not in the motive, but in the power of willing itself.

OBJECTION--PARTICULAR VOLITION, HOW ACCOUNTED FOR.

III. We are also prepared to notice the great objection of Necessitarians to the doctrine of Liberty as here maintained. How, it is asked, shall we account, on this theory, for particular volitions? The power to will only accounts for acts of Will in some direction, but not for one act in distinction from another. This distinction must be accounted for, or we have an event without a cause. To this argument I reply,

1. It assumes the position in debate, to wit: that there cannot be consequents which are not necessarily connected with particular antecedents, which antecedents necessitate these particular consequents in distinction from all others.

2. To account for any effect, all that can properly be required is, to assign the existence and operation of a cause adequate to the production of such effects. Free-agency itself is such a cause in the case now under consideration. We have here given the existence and operation of a cause which must produce one of two effects, and is equally capable, under the circumstances, of producing either. Such a cause accounts for the existence of such an effect, just as much as the assignment of an antecedent necessarily producing certain consequents, accounts for those consequents.

3. If, as this objection affirms, an act of Will, when there is no perceived or felt reason for that act in distinction from every other, is equivalent to an event without a cause; then it would be as impossible for us to conceive of the former as of the latter. We cannot even conceive of an event without a cause. But we can conceive of an act of Will when no reason, but the power of willing, exists for that particular act in distinction from others. We cannot conceive of an event without a cause. But we can conceive of the mind's selecting odd, for example, instead of even, without the Intellect or Sensibility impelling the Will to that act in distinction from others. Such act, therefore, is not equivalent to an event without a cause. The objection under consideration is consequently wholly baseless.

FACTS LIKE THE ABOVE WRONGLY ACCOUNTED FOR.

IV. The manner in which Necessitarians sometimes endeavor to account for acts of Will in which a selection is made between objects perceived and felt to be perfectly equal, requires attention. Suppose that A and B are before the mind. One or the other is to be selected, or no selection at all is to be made. These objects are present to the mind as perfectly equal. The Intelligence and Sensibility are in a state of entire equilibrium between them. Now when one of these objects is selected in distinction from the other, this act of Will is to be accounted for, it is said, by referring back to the determination to make the selection instead of not making it. The Will does not choose between A and B, at all. The choice is between choosing and not choosing. But mark: To determine to select A or B is one thing. To select one in distinction from the other, is quite another. The former act does not determine the Will towards either in distinction from the other. This last act remains to be accounted for. When we attempt to account for it, we cannot do it, by referring to the Intelligence or Sensibility for these are in a state of perfect equilibrium between the objects. We can account for it only by falling back upon the power of willing itself, and admitting that the Will is free, and not subject to the law of Necessity.

CHOOSING BETWEEN OBJECTS KNOWN TO BE EQUAL--HOW TREATED BY NECESSITARIANS.

V. The manner in which Necessitarians treat facts of this kind, to wit, choosing between things perceived and felt to be equal, also demands a passing notice. Such facts are of very little importance, one way or the other, they say, in mental science. It is the height of folly to appeal to them to determine questions of such moment as the doctrine of Liberty and Necessity. I answer: Such facts are just as important in mental science, as the fall of a piece of gold and a feather, in an exhausted receiver, is in Natural Philosophy. The latter reveals with perfect clearness the great law of attraction in the material universe. The former reveals with equal conspicuousness the great law of Liberty in the realm of mind. The Necessitarian affirms, that no act of Will is possible, only in the direction of the dictates of the Intelligence, or of the strongest impulse of the Sensibility. Facts are adduced in which, from the necessity of the case, both Faculties must be in a state of perfect equilibrium. Neither can impel the Will in one direction, in distinction from the other. In such circumstances, if the doctrine of Necessity is true, no acts of Will are possible. In precisely these circumstances acts of Will do arise. The doctrine of Necessity therefore is overthrown, and the truth of that Liberty is demonstrated. So important are those facts which Necessitarians affect to despise. True philosophy, it should be remembered, never looks contemptuously upon facts of any kind.

PALPABLE MISTAKE.

VI. We are prepared to notice a palpable mistake into which Necessitarians have fallen in respect to the use which the advocates of the doctrine of Liberty design to make of the fact, that the Will can and does select between objects perceived and felt to be equal.

"The reason why some metaphysical writers," says President Day, "have laid so much stress upon this apparently insignificant point, is probably the inference which they propose to draw from the position which they assume. If it be conceded that the mind decides one way or the other indifferently, when the motives on each side are perfectly equal, they infer that this may be the fact, in all other cases, even though the motives to opposite choices may be ever so unequal. But on what ground is this conclusion warranted? If a man is entirely indifferent which of two barley-corns to take, does it follow that he will be indifferent whether to accept of a guinea or a farthing; whether to possess an estate or a trinket?" The advocates of the doctrine of Liberty design to make, and do make, no such use of the facts under consideration, as is here attributed to them. They never argue that, because the Will can select between A and B, when they are perceived and felt to be equal, therefore, when the Will acts in one direction, in distinction from another, it is always, up to the moment of such action, impelled in different directions by feelings and judgments equally strong. What they do argue from such facts is, that the Will is subject to the law of Liberty and not to that of Necessity. If the Will is subject to the latter, then, when impelled in different directions by Motives equally strong (as in the cases above cited), it could no more act in the direction of one in distinction from the other, than a heavy body can move east instead of west, when drawn in each direction by forces perfectly equal. If the Will is subject to the law of Necessity, then, in all instances of selection between objects known and felt to be equal, we have an event without a cause. Even the Necessitarians, many of them at least, dare not deny that, under these very circumstances, selection does take place. They must, therefore, abandon their theory, or admit the dogma, of events without causes.

CHAPTER VI.

CONNECTION OF THE DOCTRINE OF LIBERTY WITH THE DIVINE PRESCIENCE.

THE argument on which Necessitarians chiefly rely, against the doctrine of Liberty, and in support of that of Necessity, is based upon the Divine prescience of human conduct. The argument runs thus: all acts of the Will, however remote in the distant future, are foreknown to God. This fact necessitates the conclusion, that such acts are in themselves certain, and, consequently, not free, but necessary. Either God cannot foreknow acts of Will, or they are necessary. The reply to this argument has already been anticipated in the Introduction. The Divine prescience is not the truth to which the appeal should be made, to determine the philosophy of the Will pre-supposed in the Bible. This I argue, for the obvious reason, that of the mode, nature, and degree, of the Divine prescience of human conduct we are profoundly ignorant. These we must know with perfect clearness, before we can affirm, with any certainty, whether this prescience is or is not consistent with the doctrine of Liberty. The Divine prescience is a truth of inspiration, and therefore a fact. The doctrine of Liberty is, as we have seen, a truth of inspiration, and therefore a fact. It is also a fact, as affirmed by the universal consciousness of man. How do we know that these two facts are not perfectly consistent with each other? How do we know but that, if we understood the mode, to say nothing of the nature and degree of the Divine prescience, we should not perceive with the utmost clearness, that this truth consists as perfectly with the doctrine of Liberty, as with that of Necessity.

If God foresees events, he foreknows them as they are, and not as they are not. If they are free and not necessary, as free and not necessary he foresees them. Having ascertained by consciousness that the acts of the Will are free, and having, from reason and revelation, determined, that God foreknows such acts, the great truth stands revealed to our mind, that God does and can foreknow human conduct, and yet man in such conduct be free; and that the mode, nature, and degree, of the former are such as most perfectly to consist with the latter.

I know with perfect distinctness, that I am now putting forth certain acts of Will. With equal distinctness I know, that such acts are not necessary, but free. My present knowledge is perfectly consistent with present freedom. How do I know but that God's foreknowledge of future acts is equally consistent with the most perfect freedom of such acts.

Perhaps a better presentation of this whole subject cannot be found than in the following extract from Jouffroy's "Introduction to Ethics." The extract, though somewhat lengthy, will well repay a most attentive perusal.

DANGER IN REASONING FROM THE MANNER IN WHICH WE FOREKNOW EVENTS TO THAT OF DIVINE PRESCIENCE.

"To begin, then, with a very simple remark: if we conceive that foreknowledge in the Divine Being acts as it does in us, we run the risk of forming a most incorrect notion of it, and consequently, of seeing a contradiction between it and liberty, that would disappear altogether had we a truer notion. Let us consider that we have not the same faculty for foreseeing the future as we have of reviewing the past; and even in cases where we do anticipate it, it is by an induction from the past. This induction may amount either to certainty, or merely to probability. It will amount to certainty when we are perfectly acquainted with necessary causes, and their law of operation. The effects of such causes in given circumstances having been determined by experience, we can predict the return of similar effects under similar circumstances with entire certainty, so long at least as the present laws of nature remain in force. It is in this way that we foresee, in most cases, the physical occurrences, whose law of operation is known to us; and such foresight would extend much further, were it not for unexpected circumstances which come in to modify the result. This induction can never go beyond probability, however, when we consider the acts of free causes; and for the very reason that they are free, and that the effects which arise from such causes are not of necessary occurrence, and do not invariably follow the same antecedent circumstances. Where the question is, then, as to the acts of any free cause, we are never able to foresee it with certainty, and induction is limited to conjectures of probability.

Such is the operation, and such are the limits of human foresight. Our minds foresee the future by induction from the past; this foresight can never attain certainty except in the case of causes and effects connected by necessary dependence; when the effects of free causes are to be anticipated, as all such effects are contingent, our foresight must be merely conjecture."

MISTAKE RESPECTING THE DIVINE PRESCIENCE.

"If, now, we attempt to attribute to the Deity the same mode of foresight of which human beings are capable, it will follow, as a strict consequence, that, as God must know exactly and completely the laws to which all the necessary causes in nature are subject--laws which change only according to his will,--he can foresee with absolute certainty all events which will take place in future. The certain foresight of effects, therefore, which is to us possible only in particular cases, and which, even then, is always liable to the limitation that the actual laws of nature are not modified,--this foresight, which, even when most sure, is limited and contingent, must be complete and absolute certainty in God, supposing his foreknowledge to be of like kind with ours.

But it is evident that, according to this hypothesis, the Deity cannot foresee with certainty the volitions of free causes any more than we can; for, as his foresight is founded, as ours is, upon the knowledge of the laws which govern causes, and as the law of free causes is precisely this, that their volitions are not necessary, God cannot calculate, any more than a human being can, the influence of motives, which, in any given case, may act upon such causes. Even his intelligence can lead no further than to conjectures, more probable, indeed, than ours, but never amounting to certainty. According to this hypothesis, we must, therefore, say either that God can foresee, certainly, the future volitions of men, and that man, therefore, is not a free being, or that man is free, and that God, therefore, cannot, any more than we can, foresee his volitions with certainty; and thus Divine prescience and human free-will are brought into direct contradiction.

But, gentlemen, why must there be this contradiction? Merely because we suppose that God foresees the future in the same way in which we foresee it; that his foreknowledge operates like our own. Now, is this, I ask, such an idea as we ought to form of Divine prescience, or such an idea as even the partisans of this system, which I am opposing, form? Have we any reason for thus imposing upon the Deity the limitation of our own feebleness? I think not.

Unendowed as we are, with any faculty of foreseeing the future, it may be difficult for us to conceive of such a faculty in God. But yet can we not from analogy form such an idea? We have now two faculties of perception--of the past by memory, of the present by observation; can we not imagine a third to exist in God--the faculty of perceiving the future, as we perceive the past? What would be the consequence? This: that God, instead of conjecturing, by induction, the acts of human beings from the laws of the causes operating upon them, would see them simply as the results of the free determinations of the will. Such perception of future acts no more implies the necessity of those actions, than the perception of similar acts in the past. To see that effects arise from certain causes is not to force causes to produce them; neither is it to compel these effects to follow. It matters not whether such a perception refers to the past, present, or future; it is merely a perception; and, therefore, far from producing the effect perceived, it even presupposes this effect already produced.

I do not pretend that this vision of what is to be is an operation of which our minds easily conceive. It is difficult to form an image of what we have never experienced; but I do assert, that the power of seeing what no longer exists is full as remarkable as that of seeing what has as yet no being, and that the reason of our readily conceiving of the former is only the fact that we are endowed with such a power: to my reason, the mystery is the same.

But whatever may or may not be in reality the mode of Divine foreknowledge, or however exact may be the image which we attempt to form of it, it always, I say,--and this is the only point I am desirous of proving,--it always remains a matter of uncertainty, which cannot be removed, whether the Divine foreknowledge is of a kind like our own, or not; and as, in the one case, there would not be the same contradiction that there is in the other, between our belief in Divine foreknowledge and human freedom, it is proved true, I think, that no one has a right to assert the existence of such a contradiction, and the necessity that human reason should choose between them."

SINGULAR INCONSISTENCY OF NECESSITARIANS.

There is no class of men who dwell with more frequency and apparent reverence, upon the truth, that "secret things belong to God," and those and those only, "that are revealed to us;" that "none by searching can find out God;" that "as the heavens are high above the earth, so are His ways above our ways, and His thoughts above our thoughts;" and that it is the height of presumption in us, to pretend to understand God's mode of knowing and acting. None are more ready to talk of mysteries in religion than they. Yet, strange as it may appear, it is nevertheless true, that their whole argument, drawn from the Divine foreknowledge, against the doctrine of Liberty, and in favor of that of Necessity, is based entirely upon the assumption that they have found out and fully understand the mode of the Divine prescience of human conduct; that they have so measured and determined the "ways and thoughts" of God, that they know that he cannot foresee any but necessary events; that among many events, all in themselves equally possible, and none of them necessary in distinction from others, he cannot foreknow which, in fact, will arise. We may properly ask the Necessitarian whence he obtained this knowledge, so vast and deep; whence he has thus "found out the Almighty to perfection?" To me, the pretension to such knowledge appears more like presumption than that deep self-distrust and humiliation which becomes the Finite in the presence of the Infinite. This knowledge has not been obtained from revelation. God has never told us that He can foresee none but necessary events. Whether He can or cannot foresee events free as well as necessary, is certainly one of the "secret things" which God has not revealed. If we admit ourselves ignorant of the mode of God's fore-knowledge of future events (and who will dare deny the existence of such ignorance in his own case?), the entire argument of the Necessitarian, based upon that fore-knowledge, in favor of his doctrine, falls to the ground at once.

NECESSITARIAN OBJECTION TO THE ABOVE ARGUMENT.

To all that has been said above, the Necessitarian brings an objection which he deems perfectly unanswerable. It is this: If actions are free in the sense maintained in this treatise, then in themselves they are uncertain. If they are still certainly known to God, they are both certain and uncertain, at the same time. True, I answer, but not in the same sense. As far as the powers of the agent are concerned, the action may be uncertain, while God at the same time may know certainly how he will exert his powers. In reference merely to the powers of the agent, the event is uncertain. In reference to the mind of God, who knows instinctively how he will exert these powers, the event is certain.

CHAPTER VII.

BEARING OF THE DOCTRINE OF LIBERTY UPON THE PURPOSES AND AGENCY OF GOD, IN RESPECT TO HUMAN CONDUCT.

ALL truth is in harmony with itself. Every particular truth is, and must be, in harmony with every other truth. If the doctrine of Necessity be assumed as true, we must take one view of the relation of God's purposes and agency in respect to the conduct of moral agents. If, on the other hand, we assume as true the doctrine of Liberty, quite another and a different view, in respect to this whole subject, must be taken. In the remarks which I have to make upon this subject, I shall assume the truth of the doctrine of Liberty, together with those of the perfect Divine Omniscience, Wisdom, and Benevolence. The question now arises, in the light of all these great truths, What relation do the Divine purposes and agency sustain to human action? In what sense does God purpose, preordain, and bring to pass, the voluntary conduct of moral agents? To this question but one answer can be given, in the light of the truths before us. God purposes human action in this sense only: He determines himself to act in a given manner, because it is wisest and best for him to act in that manner, and in that manner only. He determines this, knowing how intelligent beings will act under the influence brought to bear upon them by the Divine conduct. He purposes and brings about, or causes human action in this sense only, that in the counsels of eternity, He, in the exercise of infinite wisdom and goodness, preordains, and at the time appointed, gives existence to the motives and influences under which moral agents do act, and in the light of which they voluntarily determine their own character and conduct.

CONCLUSIONS FROM THE ABOVE.

GODS PURPOSES CONSISTENT WITH THE LIBERTY OF CREATURES.

1. We perceive the perfect consistency of God's purposes and agency with human liberty. If the motives and influences in view of which men do act, do not destroy their free agency,--a fact which must be true from the nature of the Will,--then God's purposes to give existence, and his agency in giving existence, to these motives and influences, cannot in any sense destroy, or interfere with such agency. This is a self-evident truth.

SENSES IN WHICH GOD PURPOSED MORAL GOOD AND EVIL.

2. We also perceive the senses in which God purposed the existence of moral good and evil, in the universe. He purposed the existence of the motives, in view of which He knew that a part of His subjects would render themselves holy, and a part would render themselves sinful. But when we contemplate all the holiness and consequent happiness which do exist, we then perceive the reason why God gave existence to these motives. The sin consequent, in the sense above explained, constitutes no part of the reason for their existence, but was always, in the Divine Mind, a reason against their existence; which reason, however, was overpowered by infinitely more important reasons on the other side. The good which results from creation and providence is the great and exclusive object of creation and providence. The evil, God always regretted, and would have prevented, if possible, i. e. if compatible with the existence of the best possible system.

DEATH OF THE INCORRIGIBLE PREORDAINED BUT NOT WILLED.

3. We also perceive the perfect consistency of those Scriptures which represent God as, on the whole, purposing the death of incorrigible transgressors, and yet as not willing it, but as willing the opposite. The purpose to destroy is based upon the foreseen incorrigibleness of the transgressor,--a purpose demanded by perfect wisdom and benevolence, in view of that foreseen incorrigibleness. The incorrigibleness itself, however, and the perdition consequent, are evils, the existence of which God never willed; but are the opposite of what he willed, are evils which a being of perfect wisdom and goodness never could, and never can will. It is with perfect consistency, therefore, that the Scriptures represent God, in view of incorrigibleness foreseen, as purposing the death of the transgressor, and at the same time, in view of the fact that such incorrigibleness is the opposite of what He wills the creature to do, as affirming, that He is not "willing that any should perish, but that all should come to a knowledge of the truth."

GOD NOT RESPONSIBLE FOR THE DEATH OF THE INCORRIGIBLE.

4. We see, also, how it is, that, while God does that, and eternally purposed to do that, in view of which he eternally knew that certain of his creatures would for ever destroy themselves, none but themselves are in fault for such destruction. The reasons are these:

(1.) God never did anything in view of which men ought to act thus, nor which did not lay them under obligations infinite, to act differently, and which was not best adapted to secure that end.

(2.) Their destruction constituted no part of the object of God in creation and providence, the opposite of this being true.

(3.) The great object of God in creation and providence was and is, to produce the greatest possible amount of holiness and consequent happiness, and to prevent, in every possible way consistent with this end, the existence of sin, and consequently of misery.--Now if creatures perish under such an influence, they perish by their own fault.

SIN A MYSTERY.

5. I have a single remark to make upon those phenomena of the Will, in which evil is chosen instead of good, or sin instead of holiness. That all intelligent beings possess the power to make such a choice, is a fact affirmed by universal consciousness. But that any being, under any circumstances, should make such a choice, and that he should for ever refuse to return to the paths of virtue, notwithstanding his experience of the consequences of sin, is an abuse of human liberty, which must for ever remain an inexplicable mystery. When a being assigns the real reason in view of which right is chosen, we are always satisfied with such reason. But we are never satisfied with the reason for the opposite course.

CONCLUSION FROM THE ABOVE.

One conclusion forces itself upon us, from that view of the Divine government which consists with the doctrine of Liberty. The aspect of that government which results from this view of the subject commends itself to the reason and conscience of the intelligent universe. Mysteries we do and must find in it; but absurdities and contradictions, never. Under such a Government, no being is condemned for what he cannot avoid, nor rewarded for what he could but do. While

"God sits on no precarious throne, Nor borrows leave to be," the destiny of the creature turns upon his own deserts, his own choice of good or evil. The elucidation of the principles of such a government "commends itself to every man's conscience in the sight of God."

CHAPTER VIII.

OBLIGATION PREDICABLE ONLY OF THE WILL.

SECTION I.

THE Will, as I have already said, exists in a trinity with the Intelligence and Sensibility. In respect to the operations of the different departments of our mental being, I lay down the two following propositions:

1. Obligation, moral desert, &c., are directly predicable only of the action of the Will.

2. For the operations of the other faculties we are accountable so far forth only as the existence and character of such operations depend upon the Will. In other words, it is for voluntary acts and states only that we are accountable. This I argue because,

1. Obligation, as we have seen, consists only with Liberty. All the phenomena of the Intelligence and Sensibility, in the circumstances of their occurrence, are not free, but necessary. Accountability, therefore, cannot be predicated of such phenomena. We may be, and are, accountable for such phenomena, so far forth as their existence and character depend upon the Will: in other words, so far forth as they are voluntary, and not involuntary, states of mind.

2. The truth of the above proposition, and of that only, really corresponds with the universal conviction of the race. This conviction is expressed in two ways.

(1.) When blame is affirmed of the operations of the Intelligence or Sensibility, it is invariably thus affirmed: "You have no right to entertain such thoughts or sentiments. You have no right indulge such feeling's." In other words, praise or blame is never directly predicated of these operations themselves, but of the action of the Will relatively to them.

(2.) All men agree, that the moral character of all actions, of all states of mind whatever; depends upon intention. In no point is there a more universal harmony among moral philosophers than in respect to this. But intention is undeniably a phenomenon of the Will, and of that exclusively. We must therefore admit, that moral obligation is predicable of the Will only, or deny the fundamental convictions of the race.

3. The truth of the above propositions is intuitively evident, the moment the mind apprehends their real import. A man, as he steps out of a warm room, amid the external frosts of winter, feels an involuntary chill over his whole system. We might with the same propriety attribute blame to him for such feelings, as for any other feelings, thoughts, or perceptions which exist alike independent of his Will, and especially in opposition to its determinations.

4. If we suppose all the voluntary acts and states of a moral agent to be, and always to have been, in perfect conformity to moral rectitude, it is impossible for us to impute moral guilt to him for any feelings or thoughts which may have risen in his mind independently of his Will. We can no more conceive him to have incurred ill desert, than we can conceive of the annihilation of space. We may safely put it to the consciousness of every man whether this is not the case. This renders demonstrably evident the truth, that moral obligation is predicable only of the Will.

5. With the above perfectly harmonize the positive teachings of Inspiration. For example. "Lust, when it is conceived, bringeth forth sin." The involuntary feeling does not constitute the sin, but the action of the Will in harmony with that feeling.

6. A single supposition will place this whole subject in a light perfectly conspicuous before the mind. We can readily conceive that the Will, or voluntary states of the mind, are in perfect harmony with the moral law, while the Sensibility, or involuntary states, are opposed to it. We can also with equal readiness make the opposite supposition, to wit, that the Sensibility, or involuntary states, are in harmony with the law, while the determinations of the Will are all opposed to it. What shall we think of these

two states? Let us suppose a case of no unfrequent occurrence, that the feelings, or involuntary state of the mind, are in perfect harmony with the law, while the action of this Will, or the voluntary states, are in determined opposition to the law, the individual being inflexibly determined to quench such feelings, and act in opposition to them. Is there any virtue at all in such a state of mind? Who would dare to say that there is? Is not the guilt of the individual aggravated in proportion to the depth and intensity of the feeling which he is endeavoring to suppress? Now if, as all will admit, there is no virtue at all, when the states of the Sensibility are in harmony with the law, and the determinations of the Will, or voluntary states of the mind, are opposed to it, how can there be guilt when the Will, or voluntary states, are in perfect harmony with the law, and the Sensibility or involuntary states, opposed to it? This renders it demonstrably evident that obligation and moral desert of praise or blame are predicable only of the Will, or voluntary states of mind.

7. We will make another supposition; one, if possible, still more to the point. The tiger, we well know, has received from his Maker, either directly or through the laws of natural generation sustained by the Most High, a ferocious nature. Why do we not blame the animal for this nature? The answer, perhaps, would be, that he is not a rational being, and is therefore not responsible for anything.

Let us suppose, then, that with this nature, God had associated Intelligence and Free-Will, such as man possesses. Why should the animal now be held responsible for the bare existence of this nature, any more than in the first instance, when the effect, in both instances, exists, alike independent of his knowledge, choice, and agency? A greater absurdity than this never lay upon the brain of a Theologian, that the mere existence of rationality renders the subject properly responsible for what God himself produces in connection with that rationality, and produces wholly independent of the knowledge, choice, and agency of that subject.

Let us suppose, further, that the animal under consideration, as soon as he becomes aware of the existence and tendencies of this nature, holds all its impulses in perfect subjection to the law of love, and never suffers them, in a single instance, to induce a voluntary act contrary to that law. Is it in the power of the Intelligence to affirm guilt of that creature? Do we not necessarily affirm his virtue to be great in proportion to the strength of the propensity thus perfectly subjected to the Moral law? The above illustration renders two conclusions demonstrably evident:

1. For the mere existence of any constitutional propensity whatever, the creature is not and cannot be responsible.

2. When all the actions of the Will, or voluntary power, are in perfect harmony with the moral law, and all the propensities are held in full subjection to that law, the creature stands perfect and complete in the discharge of his duty to God and Man. For the involuntary and necessary actings of those propensities, he cannot be responsible.

It is no part of my object to prove that men have not derived from their progenitors, propensities which impel and induce them to sin; but that, for the mere existence of these propensities, together with their necessary involuntary action, they are not guilty.

SEC. II. DOGMAS IN THEOLOGY.

Certain dogmas in Theology connected with the subject above illustrated here claim our attention.

MEN NOT RESPONSIBLE FOR THE SIN OF THEIR PROGENITORS.

I. The first that I notice is the position, that creatures are now held responsible, even as "deserving God's wrath and curse, not only in this life, but in that which is to come," not merely for their own voluntary acts of disobedience, nor for their involuntary exercises, but for the act of a progenitor, performed when they had no existence. If God holds creatures responsible for such an act, we may safely affirm that it is absolutely impossible for them to conceive of the justice of such a principle; and that God has so constituted them, as to render it impossible for them to form such a conception. Can a being who is not a moral agent sin? Is not existence necessary to moral agency? How then can creatures "sin in and through another" six thousand years before their own existence commenced? We cannot conceive of creatures as guilty for the involuntary and necessary exercises of their own minds. How can we conceive of them as guilty for the act of another being,--an act of which they had, and could have, no knowledge, choice, or agency whatever? How can intelligent beings hold such a dogma, and hold it as a revelation from Him who has declared with an oath, that the "son shall not bear the iniquity of the father," but that "every man shall die for his own sins?"

CONSTITUTIONAL ILL-DESERT.

II. The next dogma deserving attention is the position, that mankind derive from our first progenitor a corrupt nature, which renders obedience to the commands of God impossible, and disobedience necessary, and that for the mere existence of this nature, men "deserve God's wrath and curse, not only in this world, but in that which is to come."

If the above dogma is true, it is demonstrably evident, that this corrupt nature comes into existence without the knowledge, choice, or agency of the creature, who, for its existence, is pronounced deserving of, and "bound over to the wrath of God." Equally evident is it, that this corrupt nature exists as the result of the direct agency of God. He proclaims himself the Maker of "every soul of man." As its Maker, He must have imparted to that soul the constitution or nature which it actually possesses. It does not help the matter at all, to say, that this nature is derived from our progenitor: for the laws of generation, by which this corrupt nature is derived from that progenitor, are sustained and continued by God himself. It is a truth of reason as well as of revelation, that, even in respect to plants, derived "by ordinary generation" from the seed of those previously existing, it is GOD who "giveth them a body as it hath pleased him, and to every seed its own body." If this is true of plants, much more must it be so of the soul of man.

If, then, the above dogma is true, man, in the first place, is held as deserving of eternal punishment for that which exists wholly independent of his knowledge, choice, or agency, in any sense, direct or indirect. He is also held responsible for the result, not of his own agency, but for that which results from the agency of God. On this dogma, I remark,

1. It is impossible for the Intelligence to affirm, or even to conceive it to be true, that a creature deserves eternal punishment for that which exists wholly independent of his knowledge, choice, or agency; for that which results, not

from his own agency, but from that of another. The Intelligence can no more affirm the truth of such propositions, than it can conceive of an event without a cause.

2. This dogma is opposed to the intuitive convictions of the race. Present the proposition to any mind, that, under the Divine government, the creature is held responsible for his own voluntary acts and states of minds only, and such a principle "commends itself to every man's conscience in the sight of God." Present the dogma, on the other hand, that for a nature which renders actual obedience impossible, a nature which exists as the exclusive result of the agency of God himself, independently of the knowledge, choice, or agency of the creature, such creature is justly "bound over to the wrath of God, and curse of the law, and so made subject to death, with all miseries, spiritual, temporal, and eternal," and there is not a conscience in the universe which will not reprobate with perfect horror such a principle. The intuitive convictions of the race are irreconcilably opposed to it.

3. If mankind, as this dogma affirms, have a nature from which voluntary acts of a given character necessarily result, to talk of real growth or confirmation in holiness or sin, is to use words without meaning. All that influence, or voluntary acts, can do in such a case, is to develope the nature already in existence. They can do nothing to confirm the soul in its tendencies, one way or the other. What should we think of the proposition, that a certain tree had formed and confirmed the habit of bearing particular kinds of fruits, when it commenced bearing, with the necessity of bearing this kind only, and with the absolute impossibility of bearing any other? So the soul, according to this dogma, commences action with the absolute impossibility of any but sinful acts, and with the equal necessity of putting forth sinful ones. Now, Necessity and Impossibility know and can know no degrees. How then can a mind, thus constituted, generate and confirm the habit of sinning? What, on this supposition, is the meaning of the declaration, "How can ye, who are accustomed to do evil, learn to do well?" All such declarations are without meaning, if this dogma is true.

4. If God imputes guilt to the creature, for the existence of the nature under consideration, he must have required the creature to prevent its existence. For it is a positive truth of reason and inspiration both, that as "sin is a transgression of the law;" that "where there is no law, there is no

transgression;" and that "sin is not imputed where there is no law," that is, where nothing is required, no obligation does or can exist, and consequently no guilt is imputed. The existence of the nature under consideration, then, is not and cannot be sin to the creature, unless it is a transgression of the law; and it cannot be a transgression of the law, unless the law required the creature to prevent its existence, and prevent it when that existence was the exclusive result of God's agency, and when the creature could have no knowledge, choice, or agency, in respect to what God was to produce. Can we conceive of a greater absurdity than that? God is about to produce a certain nature by his own creative act, or by sustaining the laws of natural generation. He imputes infinite guilt to the creature for not preventing the result of that act, and inducing a result precisely opposite, and that in the absence of all knowledge of what was required of him, and of the possibility of any agency in respect to it. Is this a true exposition of the Government of God?

PRESENT IMPOSSIBILITIES REQUIRED.

III. The last dogma that I notice is the position, that the Moral law demands of us, as sinners, not what is now possible to us on the ground of natural powers and proffered grace, but what would be possible, had we never sinned. It is admitted by all, that we have not now a capacity for that degree of virtue which would be possible to us, had we always developed our moral powers in harmony with the Divine law. Still it is maintained, that this degree of virtue, notwithstanding our present total incapacity to exercise it, is demanded of us. For not rendering it, we are justly bound over to the wrath and curse of God. In reply, I remark:

1. That this dogma, which is professedly founded on the express teachings of Inspiration, has not even the shadow of a foundation in any direct or implied affirmation of the Bible. I may safely challenge the world to adduce a single passage of Holy Writ, that either directly or indirectly asserts any such thing.

2. This dogma is opposed not only to the spirit, but to the letter of the law. The law, addressing men, enfeebled as their powers now are, in consequence of sin previously committed, requires them to love God with all their "mind and strength," that is, not with the power they would have possessed, had they never sinned, but with the power they now actually possess. On what

authority does any Theologian affirm, when the law expressly makes one demand upon men, that it, in reality, makes another, and different demand? In such an assertion, is he not wise, not only above, but against what is written?

3. This dogma is opposed to the express and positive teachings of Inspiration. The Scriptures expressly affirm, Rom. xiii. 8, that every one that exercises love, "hath fulfilled the law," hath done all that the law requires of him. This would not be true, did the law require a degree of love not now practicable to the creature. Again, in Deut. x. 12, it is positively affirmed, that God requires nothing of his creatures but to "love him with all the heart and with all the soul," that is, with all the powers they actually possess. This could not be true, if the dogma under consideration is true.

4. If we conceive an individual to yield a voluntary conformity to moral obligations of every kind, to the full extent of his present capacities, it is impossible for us to conceive that he is not now doing all that he really ought to do. No person would ever think of exhorting him to do more, nor of charging him with guilt for not doing it. We may properly blame him for the past, but as far as the present is concerned, he stands guiltless in the eye of reason and revelation both.

5. Let us suppose that an individual continues for fifty years in sin. He is then truly converted, and immediately after dies. All admit that he enters heaven in a state of perfect holiness. Yet no one supposes that he now exercises, or has the capacity to exercise, as high a degree of holiness, as he would, had he spent those fifty years in obedience, instead of disobedience to God. This shows that even those who theoretically hold the dogma under consideration do not practically believe it themselves.

The conclusion to which our inquiries lead us is this: Holiness is a voluntary conformity to all perceivable obligation. Sin is a similar violation of such obligation. Nothing else is or can be holiness. Nothing else is or can be sin.

CHAPTER IX.

THE STANDARD BY WHICH THE MORAL CHARACTER OF VOLUNTARY STATES OF MIND, OR ACTS OF WILL, SHOULD BE DETERMINED.

IN the remarks which I have to make in elucidation of this subject, I shall, on the authority of evidence already presented, take two positions for granted:

1. Moral obligation and moral desert are predicable only of acts of Will.

2. It is only of those acts of Will denominated Intentions, and of course ultimate intentions, that obligation, merit and demerit, are predicable.

In this last position, as I have already said, there is a universal agreement among moral philosophers. We may also safely assume the same as a first truth of the universal Intelligence. The child, the philosopher, the peasant, men of all classes, ages, and conditions, agree in predicating obligation and moral desert of intention, and of ultimate intention only. By ultimate intention, I, of course, refer to those acts, choices, or determinations of the Will, to which all other mental determinations are subordinate, and by which they are controlled. Thus, when an individual chooses, on the one hand, the Divine glory, and the highest good of universal being, as the end of his existence; or, on the other, his own personal gratification; and subordinates to one or the other of these acts of choice all the law of his being, here we find his ultimate intention. In this exclusively all mankind agree in finding the moral character of all mental acts and states.

Now an important question arises, By what standard shall we judge of the moral character of intentions? Of course, they are to be placed in the light of the two great precepts of the Moral law by which we are required to love God with all our powers, and our neighbor as ourselves. But two distinct and opposite explanations have been given of the above precepts, presenting entirely different standards of moral judgment. According to one, the precept requiring us to love God with all our heart and strength, requires a certain degree of intensity of intention and feeling. On no other condition, it is said, do we love God with all the heart.

According to the other explanation, the precept requiring us to love God with all the heart, &c., means, that we devote our entire powers and interests to the glory of God and the good of his creatures, with the sincere intention to employ these powers and interests for the accomplishment of these objects in the best possible manner. When all our powers are under the exclusive control of such an intention as this, we then, it is affirmed, love God according to the letter and spirit of the above precept, "with all our heart, and with all our strength."

SINCERITY, AND NOT INTENSITY, THE TRUE STANDARD.

My object now is to show, that this last is the right exposition, and presents the only true standard by which to judge of all moral acts and states of mind. This I argue from the following considerations.

1. If intensity be fixed upon as the standard, no one can define it, so as to tell us what he means. The command requiring us to love with all the heart, if understood as requiring a certain degree of intensity of intention, may mean the highest degree of tension of which our nature is susceptible. Or it may mean the highest possible degree, consistent with our existence in this body; or the highest degree consistent with the most perfect health; or some inconceivable indefinable degree, nobody knows what. It cannot include all, and may and must mean some one of the above-named dogmas. Yet no one would dare to tell us which. Has God given, or does our own reason give us, a standard of moral judgment of which no one can form a conception, or give us a definition?

2. No one could practically apply this standard, if he could define it, as a test of moral action. The reason is obvious. No one, but Omniscience, can possibly know what degree of tensity our nature is capable of; nor precisely what degree is compatible with life, or with the most perfect health. If intensity, then, is the standard by which we are required to determine definitely the character of moral actions, we are in reality required to fix definitely the value of an unknown quantity, to wit: moral action, by a standard of which we are, and of necessity must be, most profoundly ignorant. We are required to find the definite by means of the indefinite; the plain by means of the "palpable obscure." Has God, or our own reason, placed us in such a predicament as this, in respect to the most momentous of all questions, the determination of our true moral character and deserts?

3. While the standard under consideration is, and must be, unknown to us, it is perpetually varying, and never fixed. The degree of intensity of mental effort of which we are capable at one moment, differs from that which is

possible to us at another. The same holds equally of that which is compatible with life and health. Can we believe that "the judge of all the earth" requires us to conform, and holds us responsible for not conforming to a standard located we cannot possibly know where, and which is always movable, and never for a moment remaining fixed?

4. The absurdity of attempting to act in conformity to this principle, in reference to particular duties, will show clearly that it cannot be the standard of moral obligations in any instance. Suppose an individual becomes convinced that it is his duty, that is, that God requires him to walk or travel a given distance, or for a time to compose himself for the purpose of sleeping. Now he must will with all his heart to perform the duty before him. What if he should judge himself bound to will to sleep, for example, and to will it with all possible intensity, or with as great an intensity as consists with his health? How long would it take him to compose himself to sleep in this manner? What if he should with all possible intensity will to walk? What if, when with all sincerity, he had intended to perform, in the best manner, the duty devolved upon him, he should inquire whether the intention possessed the requisite intensity? It would be just as rational to apply this standard in the instances under consideration, as in any other.

5. That Sincerity, and not intensity of intention, presents the true standard of moral judgment, is evident from the fact, that the former commends itself to every man's conscience as perfectly intelligible, of ready definition in itself, and of consequently ready application, in determining the character and moral desert of all moral actions. We can readily conceive what it is to yield all our powers and interests to the Will of God, and to do it with the sincere intention of employing them in the wisest and best manner for the accomplishment of the highest good. We can conceive, too, what it is to employ our powers and interests under the control of such an intention. We can also perceive with perfect distinctness our obligation to live and act under the supreme control of such an intention. If we are bound to yield to God at all, we are bound to yield our entire being to his supreme control. If we are bound to will and employ our powers and resources to produce any good at all, we are bound to will and aim to produce the highest good.

This principle also is equally applicable in, determining the character and deserts of all moral actions. Every honest mind can readily determine the fact, whether it is or is not acting under the supreme control of the intention under consideration. If we adopt this principle, as expressing the meaning of the command requiring us to love with all the heart, perfect sunlight rests upon the Divine law. If we adopt any other standard, perfect midnight hangs over that law.

6. If we conceive a moral agent really to live and act in full harmony with the intention under consideration, it is impossible for us to conceive, or affirm, that he has not done his entire duty. What more ought a moral agent to intend than the highest good he can accomplish? Should it be said, that he ought to intend this with a certain degree of intensity, the reply is, that Sincerity implies an intention to will and act, at all times, with that degree of intensity best adapted to the end to be accomplished. What more can properly or wisely be demanded? Is not this loving with all the heart?

7. On this principle, a much greater degree of intensity, and consequent energy of action, will be secured, than on the other principle. Nothing tends more effectually to palsy the energies of the mind, than the attempt always to act with the greatest intensity. It is precisely like the attempt of some orators, to speak, on all subjects alike, with the greatest possible pathos and sublimity. On the other hand, let an individual throw his whole being under the control of the grand principle of doing all the good he can, and his powers will energize with the greatest freedom, intensity, and effect. If, therefore, the standard of moral obligation and moral desert has been wisely fixed, Sincerity, and nothing else, is that standard.

8. I remark, once more, that Sincerity is the standard fixed in the Scriptures of truth. In Jer. iii. 16, the Jews are accused of not "turning to the Lord with the whole heart, but feignedly," that is, with insincerity. If they had turned sincerely, they would, according to this passage, have done it with the whole heart. The whole heart, then, according to the express teachings of the Bible, is synonymous with Sincerity and Sincerity according to the above definition of the term. This is the true standard, according to revelation as well as reason. I have other arguments, equally conclusive as the above, to present, but these are sufficient. The importance of the subject, together with its decisive bearing upon the momentous question to be discussed in the next Chapter, is my apology for dwelling thus long upon it.

CHAPTER X.

INTUITIONS, OR MORAL ACTS, NEVER OF A MIXED CHARACTER; THAT IS, PARTLY RIGHT AND PARTLY WRONG.

WE are now prepared to consider the question, whether each moral act, or exercise, is not always of a character purely unmixed? In other words, whether every such act, or intention, is not always perfectly right or perfectly wrong I would here be understood to speak of single acts, or intuitions, in distinction from a series, which continues through some definite period, as an hour or a day. Such series of acts may, of course, be of a mixed character; that is, it may be made up of individual acts, some of which are right and some wrong. But the question is, can distinct, opposite, and contradictory elements, such as sin and holiness, right and wrong, selfishness and benevolence, enter into one and the same act No one will pretend that an individual is virtuous at all, unless he intends obedience to the moral law. The question is, can an individual intend to obey and to disobey the law, in one and the same act? On this question I remark,

1. That the principle established in the last Chapter really settles the question. No one, to my knowledge, pretends, that, as far as sincerity is concerned, the same moral act can be of a mixed character. Very few, if any, will be guilty of the folly of maintaining, that an individual can sincerely intend to obey and to disobey the law at one and the same time. When such act is contemplated in this point of light, it is almost universally admitted that it cannot be of a mixed character. But then another test is applied--that of intensity. It is conceivable, at least, it is said, that the intention might possess a higher degree of intensity than it does possess. It is, therefore, pronounced defective. On the same supposition, every moral act in existence might be pronounced defective. For we can, at least, conceive, that it might possess a higher degree of intensity. It has been abundantly established in the last Chapter, however, that there is no such test of moral actions as this, a test authorized either by reason or revelation. Sincerity is the only standard by which to determine the character and deserts of all moral acts and states. In the light of this standard, it is intuitively evident, that no one act can combine such contradictory and opposite elements as sin and holiness, right and wrong, an intention to obey and to disobey the moral law.

2. The opinions and reasonings of distinguished philosophers and theologians on the subject may be adduced in confirmation of the doctrine under consideration. Let it be borne in mind, that if the same act embraces such contradictory and opposite elements as sin and holiness, it must be, in reality, opposed to itself, one element constituting the act, being in harmony with the law, and in opposition to the other element which is opposed to the law.

Now the remark of Edwards upon this subject demands our special attention. "It is absurd," he says, "to suppose the same individual Will to oppose itself in its present act; or the present choice to be opposite to and resisting present choice; as absurd as it is to talk of two contrary motions in the same moving body at the same time." Does not the common sense of the race affirm the truth of this statement Sin and holiness cannot enter into the same act, unless it embraces a serious intention to obey and not to obey the moral law at the same time. Is not this, in the language of Edwards, as "absurd as it is to talk of two contrary motions in the same moving body at the same time."

Equally conclusive is the argument of Kant upon the same subject. Having shown that mankind are divided into two classes, the morally good and the morally evil; that the distinguishing characteristic of the former is, that they have adopted the Moral law as their maxim, that is, that it is their serious intention to comply with all the claims of the law; and of the latter, that they have not adopted the law as their maxim; he adds, "The sentiment of mankind is, therefore, never indifferent relatively to the law, and he never can be neither good nor evil." Then follows the paragraph to which special attention is invited. "In like manner, mankind cannot be, in some points of character, morally good, while he is, at the same time, in others evil; for, is he in any point good, then the moral law is his maxim (that is, it is his serious intention to obey the law in the length and breadth of its claims); but is he likewise, at the same time, in some points bad, then quoad [as to] these, the Moral law is not his maxim, (that is, in these particulars, it is his intention not to obey the law). But since the law is one and universal, and as it commands in one act of life, so in all, then the maxim referring to it would be, at the same time universal and particular, which is a contradiction;" (that is, it would be his intention to obey the law universally, and at the same time, not to obey it in certain particulars, one of the most palpable contradictions conceivable.) To my mind the above argument has all the force of demonstration. Let it be borne in mind, that no man is morally good at all, unless it is his intention to obey the Moral law universally. This being his intention, the law has no higher claims upon him. Its full demands are, and must be, met in that intention. For what can the law require more, than that the voluntary powers shall be in full harmony with its demands, which is always true, when there is a sincere intention to obey the law universally. Now, with this intention, there can be nothing in the individual morally evil; unless there is, at the same time, an intention not to obey the law in certain particulars; that is, not to obey it universally. A mixed moral act, or intention, therefore, is possible, only on this condition, that it shall embrace these two contradictory elements--a serious determination to obey the law universally, and a determination equally decisive, at the same time, to disobey it in certain particulars; that is, not to obey it universally. I leave it with the advocates of the doctrine of Mixed Moral Action to dispose of this difficulty as they can.

3. If we could conceive of a moral act of a mixed character, the Moral law could not recognize it as holy at all. It presents but one scale by which to determine the character of moral acts, the command requiring us to love with all the heart. It knows such acts only as conformed, or not conformed, to this command. The mixed action, if it could exist, would, in the light of the Moral law, be placed among the not-conformed, just as much as those which are exclusively sinful. The Moral law does not present two scales, according to one of which actions are classed as conformed or not-conformed, and according to the other, as partly conformed and partly not-conformed. Such a scale as this last is unknown in the circle of revealed truth. The Moral law presents us but one scale. Those acts which are in full conformity to its demands, it puts down as holy. Those not thus conformed, it puts down as sinful; as holy or sinful is the only light in which actions stand according to the law.

4. Mixed actions, if they could exist, are as positively prohibited by the law, and must therefore be placed under the category of total disobedience, just as much as those which are in themselves entirely sinful. While the law requires us to love with all the heart, it positively prohibits everything short of this. The individual, therefore, who puts forth an act of a mixed character, puts forth an act as totally and positively prohibited as the man who puts

forth a totally sinful one. Both alike must be placed under the category of total disobedience. A father requires his two sons to go to the distance of ten rods, and positively prohibits their stopping short of the distance required. One determines to go nine rods, and there to stop. The other determines not to move at all. One has put forth an act of total disobedience just as much as the other. So of all moral acts which stop short of loving with all the heart.

5. A moral act of a mixed character cannot possibly proceed from that regard to moral obligation which is an essential condition of the existence of any degree of virtue at all. Virtue, in no degree, can exist, except from a sacred regard to moral obligation. The individual who thus regards moral obligation in one degree, will regard it equally in all degrees. The individual, therefore, who, from such regard, yields to the claims of the law at all, will and must conform to the full measure of its demands. He cannot be in voluntary opposition to any one demand of that law. A mixed moral act, then, cannot possibly proceed from that regard to moral obligation which is the essential condition of holiness in any degree. This leads me to remark,

6. That a moral act of a mixed character, if it could exist, could arise from none other than the most purely selfish and wicked intention conceivable. Three positions, we will suppose, are before the mind--a state of perfect conformity to the law, a state of total disobedience, and a third state combining the elements of obedience and disobedience. By a voluntary act of moral election, an individual places himself in the last state, in distinction from each of the others. What must have been his intention in so doing? He cannot have acted from a regard to moral rectitude. In that case, he would have elected the state of total obedience. His intention must have been to secure, at the same time, the reward of holiness and the "pleasures of sin"--a most selfish and wicked state surely. The supposition of a moral act, that is, intention combining the elements of holiness and sin--is as great an absurdity as the supposition, that a circle has become a square, without losing any of its properties as a circle.

7. I remark again that the doctrine of mixed moral action is contradicted by the express teachings of inspiration. "Whosoever cometh after me," says Christ, "and forsaketh not all that he hath, he cannot be my disciple." The Bible knows men only as the disciples, or not disciples, of Christ. All who really comply with the condition above named are His disciples. All others,

however near their compliance, are not His disciples, any more than those who have not conformed in any degree. If an individual has really conformed to this condition, he has surely done his entire duty. He has loved with all his heart. What other meaning can we attach to the phrase, "forsaketh all that he hath?" All persons who have not complied with this principle are declared to be wholly without the circle of discipleship. What is this, but a positive assertion, that a moral action of a mixed character is an impossibility?

Again. "No man can serve two masters." "Ye cannot serve God and mammon." Let us suppose that we can put forth intentions of a mixed character--intentions partly sinful and partly holy. So far as they are in harmony with the law, we serve God. So far as they are not in harmony with the law, we serve Mammon. Now, if all our moral exercises can be of a mixed character, then it is true that, at every period of our lives, we can serve God and Mammon. The service which we can render also to each, may be in every conceivable degree. We may render, for example, ninety-nine degrees of service to God and one to Mammon, or ninety-nine to Mammon and one to God. Or our service may be equally divided between the two. Can we conceive of a greater absurdity than this?

What also is the meaning of such declarations as this, "no fountain can send forth both sweet water and bitter," if the heart of man may exercise intentions combining such elements as sin and holiness? Declarations of a similar kind abound in the Bible. They are surely without meaning, if the doctrine of Mixed Moral Actions is true.

8. Finally. It may be questioned whether the whole range of error presents a dogma of more pernicious tendency than the doctrine of Mixed Moral Actions. It teaches moral agents that they may be selfish in all their moral exercises, and yet have enough of moral purity mingled with them to secure acceptance with the "Judge of all the earth." A man who has adopted such a principle will almost never, whatever his course of life may be, seem to himself to be destitute of real virtue. He will always seem to himself to possess enough of it, to render his acceptance with God certain. The kind of virtue which can mingle itself with selfishness and sin in individual intentions or moral acts, may be possessed, in different degrees, by the worst men on earth. If this be assumed as real holiness--that holiness which will stand the ordeal of eternity, who will, who should conceive himself destitute of a title

to heaven? Here is the fatal rock on which myriads of minds are wrecked for ever. Let it ever be borne in mind, that the same fountain cannot, at the same time and place, "send forth both sweet water and bitter." "Ye cannot serve God and Mammon."

OBJECTIONS.

Two or three objections to the doctrine above established demand a passing notice here.

AN ACT OF WILL MAY RESULT FROM A VARIETY OF MOTIVES.

1. It is said that the mind may act under the influence of a great variety of motives at one and the same time. The same intention, therefore, may be the result of different and opposite motives, and as a consequence, combine the elements of good and evil. In reply, I remark, that when the Will is in harmony with the Moral law, it respects the good and rejects the bad, alike in all the motives presented. The opposite is true when it is not in harmony with the law. The same regard or disregard for moral obligation which will induce an individual to reject the evil and choose the good, or to make an opposite choice, in respect to one motive, will induce the same in respect to all other motives present at the same time. A mixed moral act can no more result from a combination of motives, than different and opposite motions can result in the same body at the same time, from forces acting upon it from different directions.

LOVING WITH GREATER INTENSITY AT ONE TIME THAN ANOTHER.

2. It is said that we are conscious of loving our friends, and serving God, with greater strength and intensity at one time than at another. Yet our love, in all such instances, is real. Love, therefore, may be real, and yet be greatly defective--that is, it may be real, and embrace elements morally wrong. It is true, that love may exist in different degrees, as far as the action of the Sensibility is concerned. It is not so, however, with love in the form of intention--intention in harmony with moral obligation, the only form of love demanded by the moral law. Such intention, in view of the same degrees of light, and under the same identical influences, cannot possess different degrees of intensity. The Will always yields, when it really does yield at all to

moral obligation, with all the intensity it is, for the time being, capable of, or the nature of the case demands.

MOMENTARY REVOLUTIONS OF CHARACTER.

3. On this theory, it is said, an individual may become perfectly good and perfectly bad, for any indefinite number of instances, in any definite period of time. This consequence, to say nothing of what is likely to take place in fact, does, as far as possibility is concerned, follow from this theory. But let us contemplate it, for a moment, in the light of an example or two. An individual, from regard to moral obligation, maintains perfect integrity of character, up to a given period of time. Then, under the influence of temptation, he tells a deliberate falsehood. Did his previous integrity so fuse itself into that lie, as to make it partly good and partly bad?--as to make it anything else than a total falsehood? Did the prior goodness of David make his acts of adultery and murder partly good and partly bad? Let the advocate of mixed moral action extract the elements of moral goodness from these acts if he can. He can just as well find these elements here, as in any other acts of disobedience to the Moral law. "The righteousness of the righteous cannot save him" from total sinfulness, any more than from condemnation "in the day of his transgression."

CHAPTER XI.

RELATION OF THE WILL TO THE INTELLIGENCE AND SENSIBILITY, IN ALL ACTS OR STATES, MORALLY RIGHT OR WRONG.

THE Will, sustaining the relation it does to the Intelligence and Sensibility, must yield itself to the control of one or the other of these departments of our nature. In all acts and states morally right, the Will is in harmony with the Intelligence, from respect to moral obligation or duty; and all the desires and propensities, all the impulses of the Sensibility, are held in strict subordination. In all acts morally wrong, the Will is controlled by the Sensibility, irrespective of the dictates of the Intelligence. Impulse, and not a regard to the just, the right, the true and the good, is the law of its action. In all such cases, as the impulses which control the Will are various, the external forms through which the internal acts, or intentions, will manifest themselves, will be equally diversified. Yet the spring of action is in all instances one and the same, impulse instead of a regard to duty. Virtue does not consist in being controlled by amiable, instead of dissocial and malign impulses, and in a consequent exterior of a corresponding beauty and loveliness. It consists in a voluntary harmony of intention with the just, the right, the true and the good from a sacred respect to moral obligation, instead of being controlled by mere impulse of any kind whatever. On the principle above illustrated, I remark:

THOSE WHO ARE OR ARE NOT TRULY VIRTUOUS, HOW DISTINGUISHED.

1. That the real distinction between those who are truly virtuous, and those who are not, now becomes apparent. It does not consist, in all instances, in the mere exterior form of action, but in the spring or intention from which all such action proceeds. In most persons, and in all, at different periods, the amiable and social propensities predominate over the dissocial and malign. Hence much of the exterior will be characterized by much that is truly beautiful and lovely. In many, also, the impulsive power of conscience--that department of the Sensibility which is correlated to the idea of right and wrong, and impels to obedience to the Moral law--is strongly developed, and may consequently take its turn in controlling the Will. In all such instances, there will be the external forms of real virtue. It is one thing, however, to put on the exterior of virtue from mere impulse, and quite another, to do the same thing from an internal respect and sacred regard for duty.

How many individuals, who may be now wearing the fairest forms of virtue, will find within them, as soon as present impulses are supplanted by the strong action of others, in opposition to rectitude, no maxims of Will, in harmony with the law of goodness, to resist and subject such impulses. Their conduct is in conformity to the requirements of virtue, not from any internal intention to be in universal harmony with moral obligation, but simply because, for the time being, the strongest impulse happens to be in that direction. No individual, it should ever be kept in mind, makes any approach to real virtue, whatever impulses he may be controlled by, till, by a sealing act of moral election, the Will is placed in harmony with the universal law of duty, and all external action of a moral character proceeds from this internal, all-controlling intention. Here we find the broad and fundamental distinction between those who are truly virtuous, and those who are not.

SELFISHNESS AND BENEVOLENCE.

2. We are also prepared to explain the real difference between Selfishness and Benevolence. The latter expresses and comprehends all the forms of real virtue of every kind and degree. The former comprehends and expresses the forms of vice or sin. Benevolence consists in the full harmony of the Will or intention with the just, the right, the true, and the good, from a regard to moral obligation. Selfishness consists in voluntary subjection to impulse, irrespective of such obligation. Whenever self-gratification is the law of action, there is pure selfishness, whatever the character or direction of the impulse may be. Selfishness has sometimes been very incorrectly defined, as a supreme regard to our own interest or happiness. If this is a correct definition, the drunkard is not selfish at all; for he sacrifices his present and future happiness, to gratify a beastly appetite, and destroys present peace in the act of self-gratification. If selfishness, however, consists in mere subjection to impulse, how supreme his selfishness at once appears! A mother who does not act from moral obligation, when under the strong influence of maternal affection, appears most distinguished in her assiduous care of her offspring. Now let this affection be crossed by some plain question of duty, so that she must violate the latter, or subject the former, and how soon will selfishness manifest itself, in the triumph of impulse over duty! A gift is not more effectual in blinding the eyes, than natural affection uncontrolled by a regard to moral obligation. Men are just as selfish, that is, as perfectly subject to the law of self-gratification, when under the influence of the social and amiable propensities, as when under that of the dissocial and malign, when, in both instances alike, impulse is the law of action. Moral agents were made, and are required to be, social and amiable, from higher principles than mere impulse.

COMMON MISTAKE.

3. I notice a mistake of fundamental importance into which many appear to have fallen, in judging of the moral character of individuals. As we have seen, when the Will is wholly controlled by the Sensibility irrespective of moral obligation, the impulsive department of conscience takes its turn, among the other propensities, in controlling the action of the voluntary power. Now because, in all such instances, there are the exterior forms of virtue, together with an apparently sincere internal regard for the same, the presence of real

virtue is consequently inferred. Now before such a conclusion can be authorized, one question needs to be determined, the spring from which such apparent virtues originate. They may arise from that regard to moral obligation which constitutes real virtue. Or they may be the result purely of excited Sensibility, which, in such instances happens to be in the direction of the forms of virtue.

DEFECTIVE FORMS OF VIRTUE.

4. Another very frequent mistake bearing upon moral character deserves a passing notice here. Men sometimes manifest, and doubtless with a consciousness of inward sincerity, a very high regard for some one or more particular principles of virtue, while they manifest an equal disregard of all other principles. Every real reform, for example, has its basis in some great principle of morality. Men often advocate, with great zeal, such reforms, together with the principle on which they rest. They talk of virtue, when called to defend that principle, of a regard to moral obligation, together with the necessity of self-sacrifice at the shrine of duty, as if respect for universal rectitude commanded the entire powers of their being. Yet but a slight observation will most clearly evince, that their regard for the right, the true, and the good, is wholly circumscribed by this one principle. Still, such persons are very likely to regard themselves as virtuous in a very high degree. In reality, however, they have not made the first approach to real virtue. Their respect for this one principle, together with its specific applications, has its spring in some other department of their nature, than a regard for what is right in itself. Otherwise their respect for what is right, would be co-extensive with the entire range of moral obligation.

SEC. II. TEST OF CONFORMITY TO MORAL PRINCIPLE.

In preceding chapters, the great truth has been fully established, that the Moral law addresses its commands and prohibitions to the Will only, and that moral obligation is predicable only of the action of the voluntary power, other states being required, only as their existence and character are conditioned on the right exercise of that power. From this, it undeniably follows, that the Moral law, in all the length and breadth of its requirements, finds its entire fulfilment within the sphere of the Will. A question of great importance here presents itself: By what test shall we determine whether the

Will is, or is not, in full harmony with the law? In the investigation of this question, we may perhaps be thought to be intruding somewhat into the domain of Moral Philosophy. Reasons of great importance, in the judgment of the writer, however, demand its introduction here.

The Moral law is presented to us through two comprehensive precepts. Yet, a moment's reflection will convince us that both these precepts have their basis in one common principle, and are, in reality, the enunciation of that one principle. The identical reason why we are bound to love God with all the heart, requires us to love our neighbors as ourselves. So the subject is presented by our Saviour himself. After speaking of the first and great commandment, He adds, "the second is like unto it," that is, it rests upon the same principle as the first.

Now the question is, What is this great principle, obedience to which implies a full discharge of all obligation, actual and conceivable; the principle which comprehends all other principles of the Moral law, and of which each particular precept is only the enunciation of this one common principle in its endlessly diversified applications? This principle has been announced in forms somewhat different, by different philosophers. I will present two or three of these forms. The first that I notice is this.

It shall be the serious intention of all moral agents to esteem and treat all persons, interests, and objects according to their perceived intrinsic and relative importance, and out of respect for their intrinsic worth, or in obedience to the idea of duty, or moral obligation.

Every one will readily apprehend, that the above is a correct enunciation of the principle under consideration. It expresses the fundamental reason why obedience to each and every moral principle is binding upon us. The reason and only reason why we are bound to love God with all the heart, is the intrinsic and relative importance of the object presented to the mind in the contemplation of the Infinite and Perfect. The reason why we are bound to love our neighbor as ourselves, is the fact, that his rights and interests are apprehended, as of the same value and sacredness as our own. In the intention under consideration, all obligation, actual and conceivable, is really met. God will occupy his appropriate place in the heart, and the creature his. No real right or interest will be dis-esteemed, and each will intentionally command that attention and regard which its intrinsic and relative importance demands. Every moral agent is under obligation infinite ever to be under the supreme control of such an intention, and no such agent can be under obligation to be or to do anything more than this.

The same principle has been announced in a form somewhat different by Kant, to wit: "So act that thy maxim of Will (intention) might become law in a system of universal moral obligation"--that is, let your controlling intention be always such, that all Intelligents may properly be required ever to be under the supreme control of the same intention.

By Cousin, the same principle is thus announced: "The moral principle being universal, the sign, the external type by which a resolution may be recognized as conformed to this principle, is the impossibility of not erecting the immediate motive (intention) of the particular act or resolution, into a maxim of universal legislation"--that is, we cannot but affirm that every moral agent in existence is bound to act from the same motive or intention.

It will readily be perceived, that each of these forms is really identical with that above announced and illustrated. It is only when we are conscious of the supreme control of the intention, to esteem and treat all persons and interests according to their intrinsic and relative importance, from respect to the idea of duty, that, in conformity with the principle as announced by Kant, our maxim of Will might become law in a system of universal legislation. When we are conscious of the control of such an intention, it is impossible for us not to affirm, according to the principle, as announced by Cousin, that all Intelligents are bound always to be under the control of the same intention. Two or three suggestions will close what I have to say on this point.

COMMON MISTAKE.

1. We notice the fundamental mistake of many philosophers and divines in treating of moral exercises, or states of mind. Such exercises are very commonly represented as consisting wholly in excited states of the Sensibility. Thus Dr. Brown represents all moral exercises and states as consisting in emotions of a given character. One of the most distinguished Professors of Theology in this country laid down this proposition, as the basis of a course of lectures on Moral Philosophy, that "everything right or wrong in a moral

agent, consists exclusively of right or wrong feelings"--feelings as distinguished from volitions as phenomena of Will. Now precisely the reverse of the above proposition is true, to wit: that nothing right or wrong, in a moral agent, consists in any states of the Sensibility irrespective of the action of the Will. Who would dare to say, when he has particular emotions, desires, or involuntary feelings, that the Moral law has no further claim upon him, that all its demands are fully met in those feelings? Who would dare to affirm, when he has any particular emotions, that all moral agents in existence are bound to have those identical feelings? If the demands of the Moral law are fully met in any states of the Sensibility--which would be true, if everything right or wrong, in moral agents, consists of right or wrong feelings--then all moral agents, at all times, and under all circumstances, are bound to have these same feelings. For what the law demands, at one time, it demands at all times. All the foundations of moral obligation are swept away by the theory under consideration.

LOVE AS REQUIRED BY THE MORAL LAW.

2. We are now prepared to state distinctly the nature of that love which is the "fulfilling of the law." It does not, as all admit, consist in the mere external act. Nor does it consist, for reasons equally obvious and universally admitted, in any mere convictions of the Intelligence. For reasons above assigned, it does not consist in any states of the Sensibility. No man, when he is conscious of such feelings, can affirm that all Intelligents are bound, under all circumstances, to have the same feelings that he now has. This would be true, if the love under consideration consists of such feelings. But when, from, a regard to the idea of duty, the whole being is voluntarily consecrated to the promotion, in the highest degree, of universal good and when, in the pursuit of this end, there is a serious intention to esteem and treat all beings and interests according to their intrinsic and relative importance; here is the love which is the fulfilling of the law. Here is the intention by which all intelligents, in reference to all interests and objects, are, at all times, bound to be controlled, and which must be imposed, as universal law, upon such Intelligents in every system of righteous moral legislation. Here is the intention, in the exercise of which all obligation is fully met. Here, consequently, is that love which is the fulfilling of the law. In a subsequent Chapter, my design is to show that this is the view of the subject presented in the Scriptures of truth. I now present it merely as a necessary truth of the

universal Intelligence.

IDENTITY OF CHARACTER AMONG ALL BEINGS MORALLY VIRTUOUS.

3. We now perceive clearly in what consists the real identity of moral character, in all Intelligents of true moral rectitude. Their occupations, forms of external deportment, and their internal convictions and feelings, may be endlessly diversified. Yet one omnipresent, all-controlling intention, an intention which is ever one and identical, directs all their moral movements. It is the intention, in the promotion of the highest good of universal being, to esteem and treat all persons and interests according to their intrinsic and relative importance, from regard to moral obligation. Thus moral virtue, in all Intelligents possessed of it, is perfectly one and identical. In this sense only are all moral agents capable of perfect identity of character. They cannot all have, at all times, or perhaps at any time, precisely the same thoughts and feelings. But they can all have, at all times, one and the same intention. The omnipresent influence and control of the intention above illustrated, constitutes a perfect identity of character in God and all beings morally pure in existence. For this reason, the supreme control of this intention implies, in all moral agents alike, a perfect fulfilment of the law, a full discharge of all obligation of every kind.

CHAPTER XII.

THE ELEMENT OF THE WILL IN COMPLEX PHENOMENA.

SECTION I.

EVERY perception, every judgment, every thought, which appears within the entire sphere of the Intelligence; every sensation, every emotion, every desire, all the states of the Sensibility, present objects for the action of the Will in one direction or another. The sphere of the Will's activity, therefore, is as extensive as the vast and almost boundless range of the Intelligence and Sensibility both. Now while all the phenomena of these two last named faculties are, in themselves, wholly destitute of moral character, the action of the Will, in the direction of such phenomena, constitutes complex states of mind, which have a positive moral character. In all instances, the moral and voluntary elements are one and identical. As the distinction under consideration has been overlooked by the great mass of philosophers and theologians, and as very great errors have thereby arisen, not only in philosophy, but in theology and morals both, I will dwell at more length upon the subject than I otherwise should have done. My remarks will be confined to the action of the Will in the direction of the natural propensities and religious affections.

ACTION OF THE WILL IN THE DIRECTION OF THE NATURAL PROPENSITIES.-- EMOTION, DESIRE, AND WISH DEFINED.

1. In respect to the action of the Will in the direction of the natural propensities, such as the appetites, the love of esteem, of power, &c., I would remark, that the complex states thence resulting, are commonly explained as simple feelings or states of the Sensibility. In presenting this subject in a proper light, the following explanations are deemed necessary. When any physical power operates upon any of the organs of sense, or when any thought is present in the Intelligence, the state of the Sensibility immediately and necessarily resulting is called a sensation or emotion. When any feeling arises impelling the Will to seek or avoid the object of that sensation or emotion, this impulsive state of the Sensibility is called a desire. When the Will concurs with the desire, a complex state of mind results, called a wish. Wish is distinguished from Desire in this, that in the former, the desire is cherished and perpetuated by the concurrence of the Will with the desire. When the Desire impels the Will towards a prohibited object, the action of the Will, in concurrence with the desire, constitutes a wish morally wrong. When the Desire impels the Will in a required direction, and the Will, from a respect to the idea of duty, concurs with the desire, a wish arises which is morally virtuous. This principle holds true in regard to the action of all the propensities. The excitement of the propensity, as a state of the Sensibility, constitutes desire--a feeling in itself destitute of all moral qualities. The action of the Will in concurrence with, or opposition to, this feeling, constitutes a complex state of mind morally right or wrong.

ANGER, PRIDE, AMBITION, &c.

Anger, for example, as prohibited by the moral law, is not a mere feeling of displeasure awakened by some injury, real or supposed, perpetrated by another. This state, on the other hand, consists in the surrendering of the Will to the control of that feeling, and thus acting from malign impulse. Pride also is not the mere desire of esteem. It consists in voluntary subjection to that propensity, seeking esteem and admiration as the great end of existence. Ambition, too, is not mere desire of power, but the voluntary surrendering of our being to the control of that propensity. The same, I repeat, holds true in respect to all the propensities. No mere excitement of the Sensibility, irrespective of the action of the Will, has any moral character. In the action of the Will in respect to such states--action which must arise in some direction under such circumstances--moral guilt, or praiseworthiness, arises.

I might here adduce other cases in illustration of the same principle; as, for example, the fact that intemperance in food and drink does not consist, as a moral act or state, in the mere strength of the appetite--that is, in the degree in which it is excited in the presence of its appropriate objects. Nor does it consist in mere excess in the quantity partaken of--excess considered as an external act. It consists, on the other hand, in the surrendering of the voluntary power to the control of the appetite. The excess referred to is the consequent and index of such voluntary subjection. The above examples, however, are abundantly sufficient to illustrate the principle.

RELIGIOUS AFFECTIONS.

2. We will now contemplate the element of the Will in those complex phenomena denominated religious affections. The position which I here assume is this, that whatever in such affections is morally right and praiseworthy, that which is directly referred to, where such affections are required of us, is the voluntary element to be found in them. The voluntary element is directly required. Other elements are required only on the ground that their existence is conditioned upon, and necessarily results from, that of the voluntary element. This must be admitted, or we must deny the position established in the last Chapter, to wit: that all the requirements of the Moral law are fully met in the right action of the Will.

SCRIPTURE TESTIMONY.

My object now is to show, that this is the light in which the subject is really presented in the Scriptures. I will cite, as examples, the three cardinal virtues of Christianity, Repentance, Love, and Faith. The question is, Are these virtues or affections, presented in the Bible as mere convictions of the Intelligence, or states of the Sensibility? Are they not, on the other hand, presented as voluntary states of mind, or as acts of Will? Are not the commands requiring them fully met in such acts?

REPENTANCE.

In regard to Repentance, I would remark, that the term is scarcely used at all in the Old Testament. Other terms and phrases are there employed to express the same thing; as for example, "Turn ye;" "Let the wicked forsake his way;" "Let him turn unto the Lord;" "He that confesseth and forsaketh his sins shall find mercy," &c. In all such passages repentance is most clearly presented as consisting exclusively of voluntary acts or intentions. The commands requiring it are, therefore, fully met in such acts. In the New Testament this virtue is distinguished from Godly Sorrow, the state of the Sensibility which accompanies its exercise. As distinguished from the action of the Sensibility, what can it be, but a voluntary state, as presented in the Old Testament? When the mind places itself in voluntary harmony with those convictions and feelings which attend a consciousness of sin as committed against God and man, this is the repentance recognized and required as such in the Bible. It does not consist in the mere conviction of sin; for then the worst of men, and even devils, would be truly repentant. Nor does it consist in the states of the Sensibility which attend such convictions; else Repentance would be Godly Sorrow, from which the Bible, as stated above, definitely distinguishes it. It must consist in a voluntary act, in which, in accordance with those convictions and feelings, the mind turns from sin to holiness, from selfishness to benevolence, from the paths of disobedience to the service of God.

LOVE.

A single passage will distinctly set before us the nature of Love as required in the Bible--that love which comprehends all other virtues, and the exercise of which is the "fulfilling of the law." "Hereby," says the sacred writer, "we perceive the love of God." The phrase "of God" is not found in the original. The passage, as it there stands, reads thus: "By this we know love;" that is, we know the nature of the love which the Scriptures require, when they affirm, that "love is the fulfilling of the law." What is that in which, according to the express teaching of inspiration, we learn the nature of this love? "Because he laid down his life for us: and we ought to lay down our lives for the brethren." In the act of "laying down his life for us," we are here told, that the love required of us is embodied and revealed. What is the nature of this love? I answer,

1. It is not a conviction of the Intelligence, nor any excited state of the Sensibility. No such thing is here referred to.

2. It does and must consist exclusively in a voluntary act, or intention. "He laid down his life for us." What is this but a voluntary act? Yet this is love, the "love which is the fulfilling of the law."

3. As an act of Will, love must consist exclusively in a voluntary devotion of our entire powers to one end, the highest good of universal being, from a regard to the idea of duty. "He laid down his life for us." "We ought to lay down our lives for the brethren." In each particular here presented, a universal principle is expressed and revealed. Christ "laid down his life for us," because he was in a state of voluntary consecration to the good of universal being. The particular act was put forth, as a means to this end. In a voluntary consecration to the same end, and as a means to this end, it is declared, that "we ought to lay down our lives for the brethren." When, therefore, the Scriptures require love of us, they do not demand the existence of particular convictions of the Intelligence, nor certain states of the Sensibility. They require the voluntary consecration of our entire being and interests to the great end of universal good. In this act of consecration, and in the employment of all our powers and interests, under the control of this one intention, we fulfil the Law. We fully discharge all obligations, actual and conceivable, that are devolved upon us. The exercise of love, like that of repentance, is attended with particular convictions and feelings. These feelings are indirectly required in the precepts demanding love, and required, because when the latter does exist, the former will of course exist.

OF FAITH.

But little need be said in explanation of the nature of Faith. It is everywhere presented in the Bible, as synonymous with trust, reposing confidence, committing our interests to God as to a "faithful Creator." Now Trust is undeniably a voluntary state of mind. "I know," says Paul, "in whom I have believed," that is, exercised faith, "that he is able to keep that which I have committed to him against that day." Here the act of committing to the care of another, which can be nothing else than an act of Will, is presented as synonymous with Faith. Faith, then, does not consist in conviction, nor in any excited feelings. It is a voluntary act, entrusting our interests to God as to a faithful Creator. The principle above established must apply to all religious affections of every kind.

SEC. II. GENERAL TOPICS SUGGESTED BY THE TRUTH ILLUSTRATED IN THE PRECEDING SECTION.

Few truths are of greater practical moment than that illustrated in the preceding section. My object, now, is to apply it to the elucidation of certain important questions which require elucidation.

CONVICTIONS, FEELINGS AND EXTERNAL ACTIONS--WHY REQUIRED, OR PROHIBITED.

1. We see why it is, that, while no mere external action, no state of the Intelligence or Sensibility, has any moral character in itself, irrespective of the action of the Will, still such acts and states are specifically and formally required or prohibited in the Bible. In such precepts the effect is put for the cause. These acts and states are required, or prohibited, as the natural and necessary results of right or wrong intentions. The thing really referred to, in such commands and prohibitions, is not the acts or states specified, but the cause of such acts and states, to wit: the right or wrong action of the Will. Suppose, that a certain loathsome disease of the body would necessarily result from certain intentions, or acts of Will. Now God might prohibit the intention which causes that disease, in either of two ways. He might specify the intention and directly prohibit that; or he might prohibit the same thing, in such a form as this: Thou shalt not have this disease. Every one will perceive that, in both prohibitions, the same thing, precisely, would be referred to and intended, to wit: the intention which sustains to the evil designed to be prevented, the relation of a cause. The same principle, precisely, holds true in respect to all external actions and states of the Intelligence and Sensibility, which are specifically required or prohibited.

OUR RESPONSIBILITY IN RESPECT TO SUCH PHENOMENA.

2. We also distinctly perceive the ground of our responsibility for the existence of external actions, and internal convictions and feelings. Whatever effects, external or internal, necessarily result, and are or may be known to result, from the right or wrong action of the Will, we may properly be held responsible for. Now, all external actions and internal convictions and feelings which are required of or prohibited to us, sustain precisely this relation to the right or wrong action of the Will. The intention being given, the effect follows as a consequence. For this reason we are held responsible for the effect.

FEELINGS HOW CONTROLLED BY THE WILL.

3. We now notice the power of control which the Will has over the feelings.

(1.) In one respect its control is unlimited. It may yield itself to the control of the feelings, or wholly withhold its concurrence.

(2.) In respect to all feelings, especially those which impel to violent or unlawful action, the Will may exert a direct influence which will either greatly modify, or totally suppress the feeling. For example, when there is an inflexible purpose of Will not to yield to angry feelings, if they should arise, and to suppress them, as soon as they appear, feelings of a violent character will not result to any great extent, whatever provocations the mind may be subject to. The same holds true of almost all feelings of every kind. Whenever they appear, if they are directly and strongly willed down, they will either be greatly modified, or totally disappear.

(3.) Over the action and states of the Sensibility the Will may exert an indirect influence which is all-powerful. If, for example, the Will is in full harmony with the infinite, the eternal, the just, the right, the true and the good, the Intelligence will, of course, be occupied with "whatsoever things are true, honest, just, pure, lovely and of good report," and the Sensibility, continually acted upon by such objects, will mirror forth, in pure emotions and desires, the pure thoughts of the Intelligence, and the hallowed purposes of the Will. The Sensibility will be wholly isolated from all feelings gross and sensual. On the other hand, let the Will be yielded to the control of impure and sensual impulse, and how gross and impure the thoughts and feelings will become. In yielding, or refusing to yield, to the supreme control of the law of Goodness, the Will really, though indirectly, determines the action of the Intelligence and Sensibility both.

(4.) To present the whole subject in a proper light, a fixed law of the affections demands special attention. A husband, for example, has pledged to his wife, not only kind intentions, but the exclusive control of those peculiar affections which constitute the basis of the marriage union. Let him cherish a proper regard for the sacredness of that pledge, and the wife will so completely and exclusively fill and command her appropriate sphere in the affections, that, under no circumstances whatever, will there be a tendency towards any other individual. The same holds true of every department of the affections, not only in respect to those which connect us with the creature, but also with the Creator. The affections the Will may control by a fixed and changeless law.

Such being the relation of the Will to the Sensibility, while it is true that there is nothing right or wrong in any feelings, irrespective of the action of the Will, still the presence of feelings impure and sensual, may be a certain indication of the wrong action of the voluntary power. In such a light their presence should always be regarded.

RELATION OF FAITH TO OTHER EXERCISES MORALLY RIGHT.

4. In the preceding Section it has been fully shown, that love, repentance, faith, and all other religious exercises, are, in their fundamental and characteristic elements, phenomena of the Will. We will now, for a few moments, contemplate the relations of these different exercises to one another, especially the relation of Faith to other exercises of a kindred character. While it is true, as has been demonstrated in a preceding Chapter, that the Will cannot at the same time put forth intentions of a contradictory character, such as sin and holiness, it is equally true, that it may simultaneously put forth acts of a homogeneous character. In view of our obligations to yield implicit obedience to God, we may purpose such obedience. In view of the fact, that, in the Gospel, grace is proffered to perfect us in our obedience, at the same time that we purpose obedience with all the heart, we may exercise implicit trust, or faith for "grace whereby we may serve God acceptably with reverence and godly fear." Now, such is

our condition as sinners, that without a revelation of this grace, we should never purpose obedience in the first instance. Without the continued influence of that grace, this purpose would not subsequently be perfected and perpetuated. The purpose is first formed in reliance upon Divine grace; and but for this grace and consequent reliance, would never have been formed. In consequence of the influence of this grace relied upon, and received by faith, this same purpose is afterwards perfected and perpetuated. Thus, we see, that the purpose of obedience is really conditioned for its existence and perpetuity upon the act of reliance upon Divine grace. The same holds true of the relation of Faith to all acts or intentions morally right or holy. One act of Will, in itself perfectly pure, is really conditioned upon another in itself equally pure. This is the doctrine of Moral Purification, or Sanctification by faith, a doctrine which is no less true, as a fact in philosophy, than as a revealed truth of inspiration.

CHAPTER XIII.

INFLUENCE OF THE WILL IN INTELLECTUAL JUDGMENTS.

MEN OFTEN VOLUNTARY IN THEIR OPINIONS.

IT is an old maxim, that the Will governs the understanding. It becomes a very important inquiry with us, To what extent, and in what sense, is this maxim true? It is undeniable, that, in many important respects, mankind are voluntary in their opinions and judgments, and therefore, responsible for them. We often hear the declaration, "You ought, or ought not, to entertain such and such opinions, to form such and such judgments." "You are bound to admit, or have no right to admit, such and such things as true." Men often speak, also, of pre-judging particular cases, and thus incurring guilt. A question may very properly be asked here, what are these opinions, judgments, admissions, pre-judgments, &c.? Are they real affirmations of the Intelligence, or are they exclusively phenomena of the Will?

ERROR NOT FROM THE INTELLIGENCE, BUT THE WILL.

The proposition which I lay down is this, that the Intelligence, in its appropriate exercise, can seldom if ever, make wrong affirmations; that wrong opinions, admissions, pre-judgments, &c., are in most, if not all instances, nothing else than phenomena, or assumptions of Will. If the Intelligence can make wrong affirmations, it is important to determine in what department of its action such affirmations may be found.

PRIMARY FACULTIES CANNOT ERR.

Let us first contemplate the action of the primary intellectual faculties-- Sense, or the faculty of external perception; Consciousness, the faculty of internal observation; and Reason, the faculty which gives us necessary and universal truths. The two former faculties give us phenomena external and internal. The latter gives us the logical antecedents of phenomena, thus perceived and affirmed, to wit: the ideas of substance, cause, space, time, &c. In the action of these faculties, surely, real error is impossible.

SO OF THE SECONDARY FACULTIES.

Let us now contemplate the action of the secondary faculties, the Understanding and Judgment. The former unites the elements given by the three primary faculties into notions of particular objects. The latter classifies these notions according to qualities perceived. Here, also, we find no place for wrong affirmations. The understanding can only combine the elements actually given by the primary faculties. The Judgment can classify only according to qualities actually perceived. Thus I might go over the entire range of the Intelligence, and show, that seldom, if ever, in its appropriate action, it can make wrong affirmations.

ERROR, WHERE FOUND.--ASSUMPTION.

Where then is the place for error, for wrong opinions, and pre-judgments? Let us suppose, that a number of individuals are observing some object at a distance from them. No qualities are given but those common to a variety of objects, such as a man, horse, ox, &c. The perceptive faculty has deceived no one in this case. It has given nothing but real qualities. The Understanding can only form a notion of it, as an object possessing these particular qualities. The Judgment can only affirm, that the qualities perceived are common to different classes of objects, and consequently, that no affirmations can be made as to what class the object perceived does belong. The Intelligence, therefore, makes no false affirmations. Still the inquiry goes round. "What is it?" One answers, "It is a man." That is my opinion. Another: "It is a horse." That is my judgment. Another still says, "I differ from you all. It is an ox." That is my notion. Now, what are these opinions, judgments, and notions? Are they real affirmations of the Intelligence? By no means. The Intelligence cannot affirm at all, under such circumstances. They are nothing in reality, but mere assumptions of the Will. A vast majority of the so called opinions, beliefs, judgments, and notions among men, and all where error is found, are nothing but assumptions of the Will.

Assumptions are sometimes based upon real affirmations of the Intelligence, and sometimes not. Suppose the individuals above referred to approach the object, till qualities are given which are peculiar to the horse. The Judgment at once classifies the object accordingly. As soon as this takes place, they all exclaim, "well, it is a horse." Here are assumptions again, but assumptions based upon real affirmations of the Intelligence. In the former instance we had assumptions based upon no such affirmations.

False assumptions do not always imply moral guilt. Much of the necessary business of life has no other basis than prudent or imprudent guessing. When the farmer, for example, casts any particular seed into the ground, it is only by balance of probabilities that he often determines, as far as he does or can determine, what is best; and not unfrequently is he necessitated to assume and act, when all probabilities are so perfectly balanced, that he can find no reasons at all for taking one course in distinction from another. Yet no moral guilt is incurred when one is necessitated to act in some direction, and when all available light has been sought and employed to determine the direction which is best.

As false assumptions, however, often involve very great moral guilt, it may be important to develope some of the distinguishing characteristics of assumptions of this class.

1. All assumptions involve moral guilt, which are in opposition to the real and positive affirmations of the Intelligence. As the Will may assume in the absence of such affirmations, and in the direction of them, so it may in opposition to them. When you have carried a man's Intellect in favor of a given proposition, it is by no means certain that you have gained his assent to its truth. He may still assume, that all the evidence presented is inadequate,

and consequently refuse to admit its truth. When the Will thus divorces itself from the Intelligence, guilt of no ordinary character is incurred. Men often express their convictions of the guilt thus incurred, by saying to individuals, "You are bound to admit that fact or proposition as true. You are already convinced. What excuse have you for not yielding to that conviction?" Yet individuals will often do fatal violence to their intellectual and moral nature, by holding on to assumptions, in reality known to be false.

2. Assumptions involve moral guilt which are formed without availing ourselves of all the light within our reach as the basis of our assumptions. For us to assume any proposition, or statement, to be true or false, in the absence of affirmations of the Intelligence, as the basis of such assumptions, when adequate light is available, involves the same criminality, as assumptions in opposition to the Intelligence. Hence we often have the expression in common life, "You had no right to form a judgment under such circumstances. You were bound, before doing it, to avail yourself of all the light within your reach."

3. Positive assumptions, without intellectual affirmations as their basis, equally positive, involve moral guilt of no ordinary character. As remarked above, we are often placed in circumstances in which we are necessitated to act in some direction, and to select some particular course without any perceived reasons in favor of that one course in distinction from another. Now while action is proper in such a condition, it is not proper to make a positive assumption that the course selected is the best. Suppose, that all the facts before my mind bearing upon the character of a neighbor, are equally consistent with the possession, on his part, of a character either good or bad. I do violence to my intellectual and moral nature, if, under such circumstances, I make the assumption that his character is either the one or the other, and especially, that it is the latter instead of the former. How often do flagrant transgressions of moral rectitude occur in such instances!

PRE-JUDGMENTS.

A few remarks are deemed requisite on this topic. A pre-judgment is an assumption, that a proposition or statement is true or false, before the facts, bearing upon the case, have been heard. Such assumptions are generally classed under the term prejudice. Thus it is said of individuals, that they are prejudiced in favor or against certain persons, sentiments, or causes. The real meaning of such statements is, that individuals have made assumptions in one direction or another, prior to a hearing of the facts of the case, and irrespective of such facts.

INTELLECT NOT DECEIVED IN PRE-JUDGMENTS.

It is commonly said, that such prejudices, or pre-judgments, blind the mind to facts of one class, and render it quick to discern those of the other, and thus lead to a real mis-direction of the Intelligence. This I think is not a correct statement of the case. Pre-judgments may, and often do, prevent all proper investigation of a subject. In this case, the Intelligence is not deceived at all. In the absence of real data, it can make no positive affirmations whatever.

So far also as pre-judgments direct attention from facts bearing upon one side of a question, and to those bearing upon the other, the Intelligence is not thereby deceived. All that it can affirm is the true bearing of the facts actually presented. In respect to those not presented, and consequently in respect to the real merits of the whole case, it makes no affirmations. If an individual forms an opinion from a partial hearing, that opinion is a mere assumption of Will, and nothing else.

THE MIND HOW INFLUENCED BY PRE-JUDGMENTS.

But the manner in which pre-judgments chiefly affect the mind in the hearing of a cause, still remains to be stated. In such pre-judgments, or assumptions, an assumption of this kind is almost invariably included, to wit: that all facts of whatever character bearing upon one side of the question, are wholly indecisive, while all others bearing upon the other side are equally decisive. In pre-judging, individuals do not merely pre-judge the real merits of the case, but the character of all the facts bearing upon it. They enter upon the investigation of a given subject, with an inflexible determination to treat all the facts and arguments they shall meet with, according to previous assumptions. Let the clearest light poured upon one side of the question, and the reply is, "After all, I am not convinced," while the most trivial circumstances conceivable bearing upon the other side, will be seized upon as perfectly decisive. In all this, we do not meet with the operations of a deceived Intelligence, but of a "deceived heart," that is, of a depraved Will, stubbornly bent upon verifying its own unauthorized, pre-formed assumptions. Such assumptions can withstand any degree of evidence whatever. The Intelligence did not give them existence, and it cannot annihilate them. They are exclusively creatures of Will, and by an act of Will, they must be dissolved, or they will remain proof against all the evidence which the tide of time can roll against them.

INFLUENCES WHICH INDUCE FALSE ASSUMPTIONS.

The influences which induce false and unauthorized assumptions, are found in the strong action of the Sensibility, in the direction of the appetites, natural affections, and the different propensities, as the love of gain, ambition, party spirit, pride of character, of opinion, &c. When the Will has long been habituated to act in the direction of a particular propensity, how difficult it is to induce the admission, or assumption, that action in that direction is wrong! The difficulty, in such cases, does not, in most instances, lie in convincing the Intelligence, but in inducing the Will to admit as true what the Intelligence really affirms.

CASES IN WHICH WE ARE APPARENTLY, THOUGH NOT REALLY, MISLED BY THE INTELLIGENCE.

As there are cases of this kind, it is important to mark some of their characteristics. Among these I cite the following:

1. The qualities of a particular object, actually perceived, as in the case above cited, may be common to a variety of classes which we know, and also to others which we do not know. On the perception of such qualities, the Intelligence will suggest those classes only which we know, while the particular object perceived may belong to a class unknown. If, in such circumstances, a positive assumption, as to what class it does belong, is made, a wrong assumption must of necessity be made. The Intelligence in this case is not deceived. It places the Will, however, in such a relation to the object, that if a positive assumption is made, it must necessarily be a wrong one. In this manner, multitudes of wrong assumptions arise.

2. When facts are before the mind, an explanation of them is often desired. In such circumstances, the Intelligence may suggest, in explanation, a number

of hypotheses, which hypotheses may be all alike false. If a positive assumption is made in such a case, it must of necessity be a false one; because it must be in the direction of some one hypothesis before the mind at the time. Here, also, the Intelligence necessitates a wrong assumption, if any is made. Yet it is not itself deceived; because it gives no positive affirmations as the basis of positive assumptions. In such circumstances, error very frequently arises.

3. Experience often occasions wrong assumptions, which are attributed incorrectly to real affirmations of the Intelligence. A friend, for example, saw an object which presented the external appearance of the apple. He had never before seen those qualities, except in connection with that class of objects. He assumed, at once, that it was a real apple; but subsequently found that it was an artificial, and not a real one. Was the Intelligence deceived in this instance? By no means. That faculty had never affirmed, that those qualities which the apple presents to the eye, never exist in connection with any other object, and consequently, that the apple must have been present in the instance given. Experience, and not a positive affirmation of the Intelligence, led to the wrong assumption in this instance. The same principle holds true, in respect to a vast number of instances that might be named.

4. Finally, the Intelligence may not only make positive affirmations in the presence of qualities perceived, but it may affirm hypothetically, that is, when a given proposition is assumed as true, the Intelligence may and will present the logical antecedents and consequents of that assumption. If the assumption is false, such will be the character of the antecedents and consequents following from it. An individual, in tracing out these antecedents and consequents, however, may mistake the hypothetical, for the real, affirmations of the Intelligence. One wrong assumption in theology or philosophy, for example, may give an entire system, all of the leading principles of which are likewise false. In tracing out, and perfecting that system, how natural the assumption, that one is following the real, and not the hypothetical, affirmations of the Intelligence! From this one source an infinity of error exists among men.

In an enlarged Treatise on mental science, the subject of the present chapter should receive a much more extensive elucidation than could be given to it in this connection. Few subjects would throw more clear light over the domains of truth and error than this, if fully and distinctly elucidated.

In conclusion, I would simply remark, that one of the highest attainments in virtue which we can conceive an intelligent being to make, consists in a continued and vigorous employment of the Intelligence in search of the right, the just, the true, and the good, in all departments of human investigation; and in a rigid discipline of the Will, to receive and treat, as true and sacred, whatever the Intelligence may present, as possessed of such characteristics, to the full subjection of all impulses in the direction of unauthorized assumptions.

CHAPTER XIV.

LIBERTY AND SERVITUDE.

LIBERTY OF WILL AS OPPOSED TO MORAL SERVITUDE.

THERE are, among others, two senses of the term Liberty, which ought to be carefully distinguished from each other. In the first sense, it stands opposed to Necessity; in the second, to what is called Moral Servitude. It is in the last sense that I propose to consider the subject in the present Chapter. What, then, is Liberty as opposed to Moral Servitude? It is that state in which the action of Will is in harmony with the Moral Law, with the idea of the right, the just, the true, and the good, while all the propensities are held in perfect subordination--a state in which the mind may purpose obedience to the law of right with the rational hope of carrying that determination into accomplishment. This state all mankind agree in calling a state of moral freedom. The individual who has attained to it, is not in servitude to any propensity whatever. He "rules his own spirit." He is the master of himself. He purposes the good, and performs it. He resolves against the evil, and avoids it. "Greater," says the maxim of ancient wisdom, "is such a man than he that taketh a city."

Moral Servitude, on the other hand, is a state in which the Will is so ensnared by the Sensibility, so habituated to subjection to the propensities, that it has so lost the prerogative of self-control, that it cannot resolve upon action in the direction of the law of right, with any rational expectation of keeping that resolution. The individual in this condition "knows the good, and approves of it, yet follows the bad." "The good that he would (purposes to do), he does not, but the evil that he would not (purposes not to do), that he does." All men agree in denominating this a state of Moral Servitude. Whenever an individual is manifestly governed by appetite, or any other propensity, by common consent, he is said to be a slave in respect to his propensities.

The reason why the former state is denominated Liberty, and the latter Servitude, is obvious. Liberty, as opposed to Servitude, is universally regarded as a good in itself. As such, it is desired and chosen. Servitude, on the other hand, may be submitted to, as the least of two evils. Yet it can never be desired and chosen, as a good in itself. Every man who is in a state of servitude, is there, in an important sense, against his Will. The state in which he is, is regarded as in itself the greatest of evils, excepting those which would arise from a vain attempt at a vindication of personal freedom.

The same principle holds true in respect to Moral Liberty and Servitude. When any individual contemplates the idea of the voluntary power rising to full dominion over impulse of every kind, and acting in sublime harmony with the pure and perfect law of rectitude, as revealed in the Intelligence, every one regards this as a state, of all others, the most to be desired and chosen as a good in itself. To enter upon this state, and to continue in it, is therefore regarded as a realization of the idea of Liberty in the highest and best sense of the term. Subjection to impulse, in opposition to the pure dictates of the Intelligence, to the loss of the high prerogative of "ruling our own spirits," on the other hand, is regarded by all men as in itself a state the most abject, and least to be desired conceivable. The individual that is there, cannot but despise his own image. He, of necessity, loathes and abhors himself. Yet he submits to self-degradation rather than endure the pain and effort of self-emancipation. No term but Servitude, together with others of a kindred import, expresses the true conception of this state. No man is in a state of Moral Servitude from choice--that is, from choice of the state as a good in itself. The state he regards as an evil in itself. Yet, in the exercise of free choice, he is there, because he submits to self-degradation rather than vindicate his right to freedom.

REMARKS.

MISTAKE OF GERMAN METAPHYSICIANS.

1. We notice a prominent and important mistake common to metaphysicians, especially of the German school, in their Treatises on the Will. Liberty of Will with them is Liberty as distinguished from Moral Servitude, and not as distinguished from Necessity. Hence, in all their works, very little light is thrown upon the great idea of Liberty, which lies at the foundation of moral obligation, to wit: Liberty as distinguished from Necessity. "A free Will," says Kant, "and a Will subjected to the Moral Law, are one and identical." A more capital error in philosophy is not often met with than this.

MORAL SERVITUDE OF THE RACE.

2. In the state of Moral Servitude above described, the Bible affirms all men to be, until they are emancipated by the influence of the Remedial System therein revealed--a truth affirmed by what every man experiences in himself, and by the entire mass of facts which the history of the race presents. Where is the individual that, unaided by an influence out of himself, has ever attained to a dominion over his own spirit? Where is the individual that, without such an influence, can resolve upon acting in harmony with the law of pure benevolence, with any rational hope of success? To meet this great want of human nature; to provide an influence adequate to its redemption, from what the Scriptures, with great propriety, call the "bondage of corruption," is a fundamental design of the Remedial System.

CHAPTER XV.

LIBERTY AND DEPENDENCE.

COMMON IMPRESSION.

A VERY common impression exists,--an impression universal among those who hold the doctrine of Necessity,--that the doctrine of Liberty, as maintained in this Treatise, renders man, really, in most important respects, independent of his Creator, and therefore, tends to induce in the mind, that spirit of haughty independence which is totally opposite and antagonistic to that spirit of humility and dependence which lies at the basis of all true piety and virtue. If this is the real tendency of this doctrine, it certainly constitutes an important objection against it. If, on the other hand, we find in the nature of this doctrine, essential elements totally destructive of the spirit of pride and self-confidence, and tending most strongly to induce the opposite spirit,-- a spirit of humility and dependence upon the grace proffered in the Remedial System; if we find, also, that the doctrine of Necessity, in many fundamental particulars, lacks these benign tendencies, we have, in such a case, the strongest evidence in favor of the former doctrine, and against the latter. The object of the present Chapter, therefore, is to elucidate the tendency of the doctrine of Liberty to destroy the spirit of pride, haughtiness, and self-dependence, and to induce the spirit of humility and dependence upon Divine Grace.

SPIRIT OF DEPENDENCE DEFINED.

Before proceeding directly to argue this question, we need to settle definitely the meaning of the phrase spirit of dependence. The conviction of our dependence is one thing. The spirit of dependence is quite another. What is this spirit? In its exercise, the mind rests in voluntary dependence upon the grace of God. The heart is fully set upon doing the right, and avoiding the wrong, while the mind is in the voluntary exercise of trust in God for "grace whereby we may serve Him acceptably." The spirit of dependence, then, implies obedience actually commenced. The question is, does the belief of the doctrine of Liberty tend intrinsically to induce the exercise of this spirit? In this respect, has it altogether a superiority over the doctrine of Necessity?

DOCTRINE OF NECESSITY TENDS NOT TO INDUCE THE SPIRIT OF DEPENDENCE.

1. In accomplishing my object, I will first consider the tendency, in this one respect, of the doctrine of Necessity. An individual, we will suppose, finds himself under influences which induce him to sin, and which consequently, if this doctrine is true, render it impossible for him, without the interposition of Divine power, not to sin. A consideration of his condition tends to convince him, that is, to induce the intellectual conviction, of his entire dependence upon Divine grace. But the intellectual conviction of our dependence, as above shown, is one thing. The spirit of dependence, which, as there stated, consists in actually trusting the Most High for grace to do what he requires,

and implies actual obedience already commenced, is quite another thing. Now the doctrine of Necessity has a tendency to produce this conviction, but none to induce the spirit of dependence: inasmuch as with this conviction, it produces another equally strong, to wit: that the creature, without a Divine interposition, will not, and cannot, exercise the spirit of dependence. In thus producing the conviction, that, under present influences, the subject does not, and cannot exercise that spirit, this doctrine tends exclusively to the annihilation of that Spirit.

When an individual is in a state of actual obedience, the tendency of this doctrine upon him is no better; since it produces the conviction, that while a Divine influence, independently of ourselves, produces in us a spirit of dependence, we shall and must exercise it; and that while it does not produce that spirit, we do not and cannot exercise it. Where is the tendency to induce a spirit of dependence, in such a conviction? According to the doctrine of Necessity, nothing but the actual interposition of Divine grace has any tendency to induce a spirit of dependence. The belief of this doctrine has no such tendency whatever. The grand mistake of the Necessitarian here, consists in the assumption, that, because his doctrine has a manifest tendency to produce the CONVICTION of dependence, it has a tendency equally manifest to induce the SPIRIT of dependence; when, in fact, it has no such tendency whatever.

2. We will now contemplate the intrinsic tendencies of the doctrine of Liberty to induce the spirit of humility and dependence. Every one will see, at once, that the consciousness of Liberty cannot itself be a ground of dependence, in respect to action, in favor of the right and in opposition to the wrong: for the possession of such Liberty, as far as the power itself is concerned, leaves us, at all times, equally liable to do the one as the other. How can an equal liability to two distinct and opposite courses, be a ground of assurance, that we shall choose the one, and avoid the other? Thus the consciousness of Liberty tends directly and intrinsically to a total annihilation of the spirit of self-dependence.

Let us now contemplate our relation to the Most High. He knows perfectly in what direction we shall, in our self-determination, exert our powers under any influence and system of influences brought to bear upon us. It is also in His power to subject us to any system of influences he pleases. He has revealed to us the great truth, that if, in the exercise of the spirit of dependence, we will trust Him for grace to do the good and avoid the evil which He requires us to do and avoid, He will subject us to a Divine influence, which shall for ever secure us in the one, and against the other. The conviction, therefore, rises with full and perfect distinctness in the mind, that, in the exercise of the spirit of dependence, action in all future time, in the direction of purity and bliss, is secure; and that, in the absence of this spirit, action, in the opposite direction, is equally certain. In the belief of the doctrine of Liberty, another truth becomes an omnipresent reality to our minds, that the exercise of this spirit, thus rendering our "calling and election sure," is, at all times, practicable to us. What then is the exclusive tendency of this doctrine? To destroy the spirit of self-dependence, on the one hand, and to induce the exercise of the opposite spirit, on the other. The doctrine of Necessity reveals the fact of dependence, but destroys the spirit, by the production of the annihilating conviction, that we neither shall nor can exercise that spirit, till God, in his sovereign dispensations, shall subject us to an influence which renders it impossible for us not to exercise it. The doctrine of Liberty reveals, with equal distinctness, the fact of dependence; and then, while it produces the hallowed conviction of the perfect practicability of the exercise of the spirit of dependence, presents motives infinitely strong, not only to induce its exercise, but to empty the mind wholly of everything opposed to it.

GOD CONTROLS ALL INFLUENCES UNDER WHICH CREATURES DO ACT.

3. While the existence and continuance of our powers of moral agency depend wholly upon the Divine Will, and while the Most High knows, with entire certainty, in what direction we shall exert our powers, under all influences, and systems of influences, brought to bear upon us, all these influences are entirely at his disposal. What tendency have such convictions, together with the consciousness of Liberty, and ability to exercise, or not to exercise, the spirit of dependence, but to induce us, in the exercise of that spirit, to throw our whole being into the petition, "Lead us not into temptation, but deliver us from evil?" If God knows perfectly under what influences action in us shall be in the direction of the right, or the wrong, and holds all such influences at his own control, what attitude becomes us in the presence of the "High and lofty One," but dependence and prayer?

4. Finally, a consciousness of a state of Moral Servitude, together with the conviction, that in the exercise of the spirit of dependence, we can rise to the "Glorious Liberty of the Sons of God;" that in the absence of this spirit, our Moral Servitude is perfectly certain; all these, together with the conviction which the belief of the doctrine of Liberty induces (to wit: that the exercise of the spirit of dependence is always practicable to us), tends only to one result, to induce the exercise of that spirit, and to the total annihilation of the opposite spirit.

While, therefore, the doctrine of Liberty sanctifies, in the mind, the feeling of obligation to do the right and avoid the wrong, a feeling which the doctrine of Necessity tends to annihilate, the former (an effect which the latter cannot produce) tends only to the annihilation of the spirit of pride and self-confidence, and to induce that spirit of filial dependence which cries "Abba, Father!"

CHAPTER XVI.

FORMATION OF CHARACTER.

ELEMENT OF WILL IN FORMATION OF CHARACTER.

CHARACTER COMMONLY HOW ACCOUNTED FOR.

IN accounting for the existence and formation of peculiarities of character, individual, social, and national, two elements only are commonly taken into consideration, the natural propensities, and the circumstances and influences under which those propensities are developed and controlled. The doctrine of Necessity permits us to take nothing else into the account. Undoubtedly, these elements have very great efficacy in determining character. In many instances, little else need to be taken into consideration, in accounting for peculiarities of character, as they exist around us, in individuals, communities, and nations.

THE VOLUNTARY ELEMENT TO BE TAKEN INTO THE ACCOUNT.

In a vast majority of cases, however, another, and altogether a different element, that of the Will, or voluntary element, must be taken into the reckoning, or we shall find ourselves wholly unable to account for peculiarities of mental and moral development, everywhere visible around us. It is an old maxim, that "every man is the arbiter of his own destiny." As character determines destiny, so the Will determines character; and man is the arbiter of his own destiny, only as he is the arbiter of his own character. The element of Free Will, therefore, must be taken into the reckoning, if we would adequately account for the peculiarities of character which the individual, social, and national history of the race presents. Even where mental and moral developments are as the propensities and external influences, still the voluntary element must be reckoned in, if we would account for facts as they exist. In a majority of instances, however, if the two elements under consideration, and these only, are taken into the account, we shall find our conclusions very wide from the truth.

AN EXAMPLE IN ILLUSTRATION.

I will take, in illustration of the above remarks, a single example--a case with which I became so familiarly acquainted, that I feel perfectly safe in vouching for the truth of the statements which I am about to make. I knew a boy who, up to the age of ten or twelve years, was under the influence of a most ungovernable temper--a temper easily and quickly excited, and which, when excited, rendered him perfectly desperate. Seldom, if ever, was he known to yield in a conflict, however superior in strength his antagonist might be. Death was always deliberately preferred to submission. During this period, he often reflected upon his condition, and frequently wished that it was otherwise. Still, with melancholy deliberation, he as often said to himself, I never can and never shall subdue this temper. At the close of this period, as he was reflecting upon the subject again, he made up his mind, with perfect fixedness of purpose, that, to the control of that temper, he would never more yield. The Will rose up in the majesty of its power, and assumed the reins of self-government, in the respect under consideration. From that moment, that temper almost never, even under the highest provocations, obtained the control of the child. A total revolution of mental developments resulted. He afterwards became as distinguished for natural amiability and self-control, in respect to his temper, as before he had been for the opposite spirit. This total revolution took place from mere prudential considerations, without any respect whatever to moral obligation.

Now suppose we attempt to account for these distinct and opposite developments of character--developments exhibited by the same individual, in these two periods--by an exclusive reference to natural propensities and external influences. What a totally inadequate and false account should we give of the facts presented! That individual is just as conscious, that it was the element of Free Will that produced this revolution, and that when he formed the determination which resulted in that revolution, he might have determined differently, as he is, or ever has been, of any mental states whatever. All the facts, also, as they lie out before us, clearly indicate, that if we leave out of the account the voluntary element, those facts must remain wholly unexplained, or a totally wrong explanation of them must be given.

The same principle holds true in all other instances. Though natural propensities and external influences greatly modify mental developments, still, the distinguishing peculiarities of character, in all instances, receive their form and coloring from the action of the voluntary power. This is true, of the peculiarities of character exhibited, not only by individuals, but communities and nations. We can never account for facts as they are, until we contemplate man, not only as possessed of Intelligence and Sensibility, but also of Free Will. All the powers and susceptibilities must be taken into the account, if men would know man as he is.

DIVERSITIES OF CHARACTER.

A few important definitions will close this Chapter.

A decisive character exists, where the Will acts in harmony with propensities strongly developed. When a number of propensities of this kind exist, action, and consequently character, may be changeable, and yet decisive.

Unity and decision of character result, when the Will steadily acts in harmony with some one over-shadowing propensity.

Character is fluctuating and changeable, when the Will surrenders itself to the control of different propensities, each easily and highly excited in the presence of its appropriate objects, and yet the excitement but temporary.

Thus, different propensities, in rapid succession, take their turn in controlling the Will.

Indecision and feebleness of character result, when the Will uniformly acts under the influence of the principle of fear and caution. To such a mind, in all important enterprises especially, there is always "a lion in the way." Such a mind, therefore, is continually in a state of distressing indecision when energetic action is necessary to success.

CHAPTER XVII.

CONCLUDING REFLECTIONS.

A FEW reflections of a general nature will conclude this Treatise.

OBJECTION. THE WILL HAS ITS LAWS.

1. An objection, often adduced, to the entire view of the subject presented in this Treatise, demands a passing notice here. All things in existence, it is said, and the Will among the rest, are governed by Laws. It is readily admitted, that all things have their laws, and that the Will is not without law. It is jumping a very long distance to a conclusion, however, to infer from such a fact, that Necessity is the only law throughout the entire domain of existence, physical and mental. What if, from the fact, that the Will has its law, it should be assumed that Liberty is that law? This assumption would be just as legitimate as the one under consideration.

OBJECTION. GOD DETHRONED FROM HIS SUPREMACY, IF THE DOCTRINE OF LIBERTY IS TRUE.

2. Another objection of a general nature, is the assumption, that the doctrine of Liberty destroys the Divine supremacy in the realm of mind. "If man," says Dr. Chalmers, "is not a necessary agent, God is a degraded sovereign." A sentiment more dishonorable to God, more fraught with fatal error, more revolting to a virtuous mind, when unperverted by a false theory, could scarcely be uttered. Let us, for a moment, contemplate the question, whether the doctrine of Liberty admits a Divine government in the realm of mind. The existence and perpetuity, as stated in a former Chapter, of free and

moral agency in creatures, depend wholly upon the Divine Will. With a perfect knowledge of the direction in which they will exert their powers, under every kind and degree of influence to which they may be subjected, He holds all these influences at his sovereign disposal. With such knowledge and resources, can God exercise no government, but that of a degraded sovereignty in the realm of mind? Can He not exercise the very sovereignty which infinite wisdom and love desire? Who would dare affirm the contrary? If the doctrine of Liberty is true, God certainly does not sit upon the throne of iron destiny, swaying the sceptre of stern fate over myriads of subjects, miscalled moral agents; subjects, all of whom are commanded, under infinite sanctions, to do the right and avoid the wrong, while subjected to influences by the Most High himself, which render obedience in some, and disobedience in others, absolute impossibilities. Still, in the light of this doctrine, God has a government in the domain of mind, a government wisely adapted to the nature of moral agents--agents capable of incurring the desert of praise or blame; a government which all approve, and under the benign influence of which, all who have not forfeited its protection by crime, may find "quietness and assurance for ever."

OBJECTION. GREAT AND GOOD MEN HAVE HELD THE DOCTRINE OF NECESSITY.

3. In reply to what has been said in respect to the tendencies of the doctrine of Necessity, the fact will doubtless be adduced, that the greatest and best of men have held this doctrine, without a development of these tendencies in their experience. My answer is, that the goodness of such men, their sense of moral obligation, &c., did not result from their theory, but existed in spite of its intrinsic tendencies. They held this doctrine in theory, and yet, from a consciousness of Liberty, they practically adopted the opposite doctrine. Here, we have the source of the deep feeling of obligation in their minds, while the intrinsic and exclusive tendency of their Theory, even in them, was to weaken and annihilate this hallowed feeling. The difference between such men and sceptics is this: The piety of the former prevents their carrying out their theory to its legitimate results; while the impiety of the latter leads them to march boldly up to those results--a fearless denial of moral obligation in every form.

LAST RESORT.

4. The final resort of certain Necessitarians, who may feel themselves wholly unable to meet the arguments adduced against their own and in favor of the opposite theory, and are determined to remain fixed in their opinions, may be readily anticipated. It is an assumption which may be expressed in language somewhat like the following: "After all, the immortal work of Edwards still lives, and will live, when those of his opponents will be lost in oblivion. That work still remains unanswered." A sweeping assumption is a very easy and summary way of disposing of a difficulty, which we might not otherwise know what to do with. Let us for a moment contemplate some of the facts which have been undeniably established in reference to this immortal work.

(1.) At the outset, Edwards stands convicted of a fundamental error in philosophy, an error which gives form and character to his whole work--the confounding of the Will with the Sensibility, and thus confounding the characteristics of the phenomena of the former faculty with those of the phenomena of the latter.

(2.) His whole work is constructed without an appeal to Consciousness, the only proper and authoritative tribunal of appeal in the case. Thus his reasonings have only an accidental bearing upon his subject.

(3.) All his fundamental conclusions have been shown to stand in direct contradiction to the plainest and most positive testimony of universal Consciousness.

(4.) His main arguments have been shown to be nothing else but reasoning in a circle. He defines, for example, the phrase "Greatest apparent good," as synonymous with choosing, and then argues, from the fact that the "Will always is as the greatest apparent good," that is, that it always chooses as it chooses, that it is subject to the law of Necessity.

So in respect to the argument from the Strongest Motive, which, by definition, is fixed upon as the Motive in the direction of which the Will, in each particular instance, acts. From the fact that the action of the Will is always in the direction of this Motive, that is, in the direction of the Motive towards which it does act, the conclusion is gravely drawn, that the Will is and must be subject, in all its determinations, to the law of Necessity. I find my mind acted upon by two opposite Motives. I cannot tell which is the strongest, from a contemplation of what is intrinsic in the Motives themselves, nor from their effects upon my Intelligence or Sensibility. I must wait till my Will has acted. From the fact of its action in the direction of one Motive, in distinction from the other, I must then draw two important conclusions. 1. The Motive, in the direction of which my Will did act, is the strongest. The evidence is, the fact of its action in that direction. 2. The Will must be subject to the law of Necessity. The proof is, the action of the Will in the direction of the Strongest Motive, that is, the Motive in the direction of which it did act. Sage argument to be regarded by Philosophers and Theologians of the 19th century, as possessing the elements of immortality!

(5.) His argument from the Divine fore-knowledge has been shown to be wholly based upon an assumption unauthorized by reason, or revelation either, to wit: that he understands the mode of that Fore-knowledge,-- an assumption which cannot be made except through ignorance, as was true in his case, without the greatest impiety and presumption.

(6.) The theory which Edwards opposes has been shown to render sacred, in all minds that hold it, the great idea of duty, of moral obligation; while the validity of that idea has never, in any age or nation, been denied, excepting on the avowed authority of his Theory.

(7.) All the arguments in proof of the doctrine of Necessity, with the single exception of that from the Divine Fore-knowledge--an argument resting, as we have seen, upon an assumption equally baseless,--involve a begging of the question at issue. Take any argument we please, with this one exception, and it will be seen at once that it has no force at all, unless the truth of the doctrine designed to be established by it, be assumed as the basis of that argument. Shall we pretend that a Theory, that has been fully demonstrated to involve, fundamentally, the errors, absurdities, and contradictions above named, has not been answered?

WILLING, AND AIMING TO PERFORM IMPOSSIBILITIES.

5. We are now prepared to answer a question about which philosophers have been somewhat divided in opinion--the question, whether the Will can

act in the direction of perceived and affirmed impossibilities? The true answer to this question, doubtless is, that the Mind may will the occurrence of a known impossibility, but it can never aim to produce such an occurrence.

The Mind, for example, while it regards the non-existence of God as that which cannot possibly occur, may come into such a relation to the Most High, that the desire shall arise that God were not. With this desire, the Will may concur, in the wish, that there were no God. Here the Mind wills a known impossibility. In a similar manner, the Mind may will its own non-existence, while it regards its occurrence, on account of its relation to the Divine Will, as impossible.

But while the Mind may thus will the occurrence of an impossibility, it never can, nor will aim, that is, intend, to produce what it regards as an impossibility. A creature may will the non-existence of God; but even a fallen Spirit, regarding the occurrence as an absolute impossibility, never did, nor will aim to annihilate the Most High. To suppose the Will to set itself to produce an occurrence regarded as impossible, involves a contradiction.

For the same reason, the Will will never set itself upon the accomplishment of that which it is perfectly assured it never shall accomplish, however sincere its efforts towards the result may be. All such results are, to the Mind, practical impossibilities. Extinguish totally in the Mind the hope of obtaining the Divine favor, and the Divine favor will never be sought. Produce in the Mind the conviction, that should it aim at the attainment of a certain end, there is an infallible certainty that it will not attain it, and the subject of that conviction will no more aim to attain that end, than he will aim to cause the same thing, at the same time, to be and not to be.

In reply, it is sometimes said, that men often aim at what they regard even as an impossible attainment. The painter, for example, aims to produce a perfect picture, while he knows well that he cannot produce one. I answer, the painter is really aiming at no such thing. He is not aiming to produce a perfect picture, which he knows he cannot, and will not produce, but to produce one as nearly perfect as he can. This is what he is really aiming at. Question the individual critically, and he will confirm what is here affirmed. Remind him of the fact, that he cannot produce a perfect picture. I know that, he replies. I am determined, however, to produce one as nearly perfect as possible. Here his real aim stands revealed. The same principle holds true in all other instances.

THOUGHT AT PARTING.

6. In taking leave of the reader, I would simply say, that if he has distinctly apprehended the great doctrine designed to be established in this Work, and has happily come to an agreement with the author in respect to it, the following hallowed impression has been left very distinctly upon his mind. While he finds himself in a state of profound and most pleasing dependence upon the Author of his being, in the Holy of Holies of the inner sanctuary of his mind, one idea, the great over-shadowing idea of the human Intelligence, has been fully sanctified--the idea of duty, of moral obligation. With the consciousness of Liberty, that idea must be to the mind an omnipresent reality. From it we can never escape and in all states, and in all worlds, it must and will be to us, as a guardian angel, or an avenging fiend. But one thing remains, and that is, through the grace proffered in the Remedial System, to "live and move, and have our being," in harmony with that idea, thus securing everlasting "quietness and assurance" in the sanctuary of our minds, and ever enduring peace and protection under, the over-shadowing perfections of the Author of our existence, and amid all the arrangements and movements of his eternal government.

FOOTNOTES

[1] See Upham on the Will, pp. 32-35.

[2] The above is a perfectly correct statement of the famous distinction between natural and moral ability made by Necessitarians. The sinner is under obligation to do right, they say, because he might do what is required of him, if he chose to do it. He has, therefore, natural but not moral power to obedience. But the choice which the sinner wants, the absence of which constitutes his moral inability, is the very thing required of him. When, therefore, the Necessitarian says, that the sinner is under obligation to obey, because he might obey if he chose to do it, the real meaning is, that the sinner is under obligation to obedience, because if he should choose to obey he would choose to obey. In other words he is under obligation to obedience, because, if he did obey, he would obey.

###

CPSIA information can be obtained at www.ICGtesting.com
Printed in the USA
LVOW10s1514090916

503836LV00071B/1301/P